HIDDEN HISTORY *of* MERIDEN

HIDDEN HISTORY *of* MERIDEN

Justin Piccirillo

Published by The History Press
An imprint of Arcadia Publishing
Charleston, SC
www.historypress.com

First published 2025

Manufactured in the United States

ISBN 9781467156301

Library of Congress Control Number: 2025943128

Notice: The information in this book is true and complete to the best of our knowledge. It is offered without guarantee on the part of the author or The History Press. The author and The History Press disclaim all liability in connection with the use of this book.

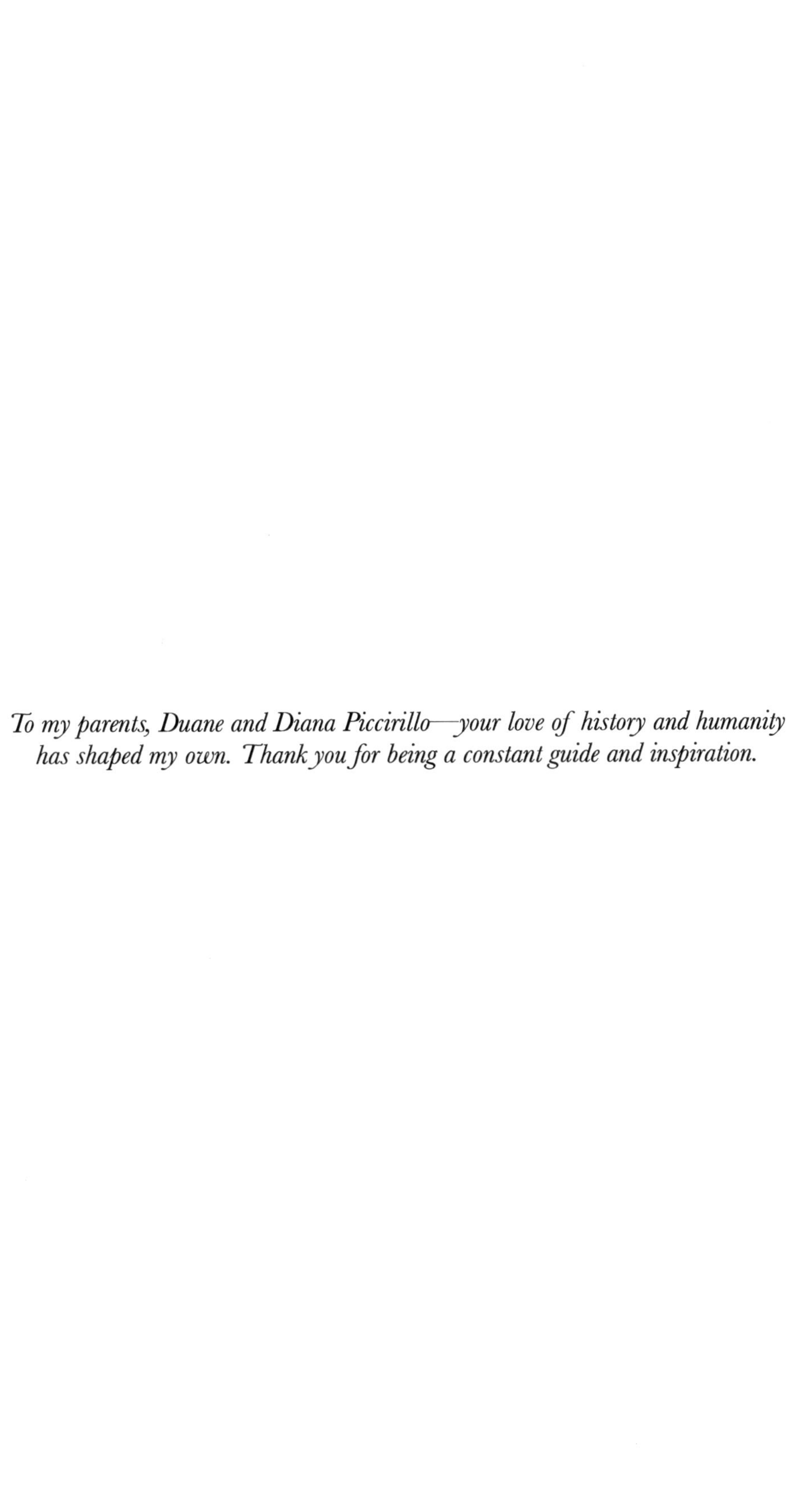

To my parents, Duane and Diana Piccirillo—your love of history and humanity has shaped my own. Thank you for being a constant guide and inspiration.

Contents

Acknowledgements

To begin, I would like to mention that every historian builds on the work of those who precede them. My study has depended, probably more than I realize, on the works of Reverend George W. Perkins, Dr. Charles Henry Stanley Davis, Frances A. Breckenridge, C. Bancroft Gillespie and George Munson Curtis, Francis Atwater, Sanford H. Wendover, Brenda J. Vumbaco and Janis Leach Franco. Each of these authors has written a suitable history of Meriden, and for that, I am grateful.

This book reflects the time, energy and expertise generously provided by a host of individuals. Chief among them are Neda and the late Allen Weathers and Sherwin and Ruth Borsuk. You selflessly opened your collections and spent many, many hours of your time helping me see this project through. Your wealth of knowledge about Meriden's past is unparalleled, and I could not have done this without each of you. For that, I am both appreciative and grateful.

I would also like to personally acknowledge the staff of the Meriden Historical Society. To Ginger Jewell, EdD, Lesley Solkoske, Chris Ruel, Chris Hendricks and the entire staff, thank you so very much for always being there when I had a question or when I needed a photograph. Your efforts are appreciated, and I am indebted to each of you.

This project would also not have been possible without the generous help of the Meriden Public Library. Thank you Becky Starr, Wanda Guzman and Prescott Hazeltine.

I am so appreciative of the brilliant photography of Lynne Vigue. Thank you for allowing me to use your captivating Meriden images time and time again. They are stunningly beautiful.

A heartfelt thank-you is also due to the following (in no particular order): Josh Cohn, Faith Twining and the staff of Edison Middle School; Seth Eddy; Cliff Monges; Keith Murphy; Ed Hanlon; Brian Cofrancesco; Arthur and Joy Dutra; Rick Dickson; Joanne Gaffney and family; Bob Beaumont and the Wallingford Historical Society; Penelope Barsch; Rob Lariviere; Chris Bourdon and the staff of the Meriden Parks and Recreation Department; Keith and JoAnne Piccirillo; Dr. Miguel Cardona; Sister Barbara, Brother Leo and Frank Critelli of the Franciscan Life Center; Mark Surowiecki; Allan and Lois Lake Church; Joe Marinan; David Emmett Cooley; Liz White Notarangelo, Eric Cotton and Erik Allison of the *Record-Journal*; Beth Dunn; Mark Zebora; Christopher R. McDowell of the Colonial Coin Collectors Club; Randy Clark; John Pagini; Josh Dummitt; Sam Carr; Krista Martino of the Meriden City Clerk's Office; Dan Murdzek; John Horne of the National Baseball Hall of Fame and Museum; Chris Barillaro; David Barillaro; Jeff Griffin; Nicholas F. Bellantoni, PhD, emeritus Connecticut state archaeologist; Linsey Walters; Suzanne Barnett; Jennifer Mooney; Chris Loos; Nicholas Pratt; Sheldon Hochheiser, PhD, corporate historian at the AT&T Archives and History Center; Brian and Rosalie Lamphier; Steven Bradley; Joanne Grabinski; Dan Larosa; Kathleen Menard; Vincent Lamberti Jr.; Lyle Brennen; Paul and Dorene Sikorski; Gary Boudreau; Vincent Mule; Frank Perzanowski; and Phil, Kelly and Luke L'Heureux.

I would also like to extend much appreciation to my editors, Michael G. Kinsella and Abigail Fleming, for their invaluable guidance and unwavering support throughout this journey.

Thank you to my parents, Duane and Diana Piccirillo, for instilling in me a great sense of local pride and historic curiosity and an enduring love for the arts.

Lastly, words cannot express my sincerest gratitude for my wife, Jennifer, and sons, Clayton, Adam and Anders, and their families. Your love, patience and encouragement have meant the world to me. I am truly grateful for your presence every step of the way.

Parish of…

I

From Farmland to Silver City

Unveiling the Early Origins and History of Meriden

Long before European settlers arrived, the land that would become Meriden was home to thriving Native American communities. The Quinnipiac and Mattabesett tribes of the Algonquian language family inhabited the region for millennia. They relied on the land for sustenance, and they practiced hunting, fishing and cultivating crops. Archaeological evidence, such as unearthed arrowheads and tools, offers a glimpse into their way of life. While it is known that these Natives never established a permanent settlement within the present-day boundaries of Meriden, their presence left an enduring mark on the landscape.

The Dutch were the first to explore Connecticut around 1614; however, the English followed shortly after and began settlements. These early settlers, most of whom were from neighboring Massachusetts, sought the economic opportunities offered by the fertile Connecticut soil. In 1636, Reverend Thomas Hooker, "the father of Connecticut," and Reverend Samuel Stone moved their congregations westward over one hundred miles from Cambridge, Massachusetts, to Hartford, which would be known as the Connecticut Colony and, later, the Connecticut River Colony. Two years later, two boatloads of English Puritans fronted by the Reverend John Davenport and Theophilus Eaton settled on the banks of Quinnipiac River in New Haven and established the New Haven Colony.

The Native Americans who resided in and around New Haven were friendly, weak and very willing to cede large tracts of land. By treaties of

Above: In the central Connecticut area, the River Tribe Indians, notably the Mattabesett and Quinnipiac, were the only Native Americans to occupy present-day Meriden. *Andy Piatek.*

Opposite: This portrait of Reverend John Davenport, a Puritan clergyman, was painted by Davenport Limner sometime around 1670. *Yale University Art Gallery.*

November and December 1638 and May 1645, Davenport and Eaton acquired a sizable area of land that stretched along the coast and inland as far as present-day Wallingford, Cheshire and parts of Bethany, Prospect, Meriden and Woodbridge. In this initial agreement on November 24, 1638, with local sachem Momaugin, the Native Americans sold all of their lands in Quinnipiac, reserving hunting and fishing rights, in return for "twelve coates of English trucking cloath, twelve alcumy spoones, twelve hatchets, twelve hoes, two dozen of knives, twelve porengers and foure cases of French knives and sizers," according to Davis's *History of Wallingford and Meriden*. By and large, the New Haven Colony treated the Indians much more fairly than was customary at that period, and amicable relations prevailed through the years.

Of the sizable tract purchased from the Native Americans, a committee from New Haven granted out lands for settling and cultivation. In 1670, Wallingford, including the greater part of present-day Meriden, was bestowed land for a new settlement on the solemn promise that the planters "live the same sort of godly community life as the parent New Haven community did," Davis noted.

It was agreed to, and as Wallingford grew, these farmers continued to expand their lots to the north, named the North Farms of Wallingford. As early as December 1724, approximately thirty-five families were living in this North Farms area of Wallingford. They were primarily farmers, and their cultivating of crops and raising livestock to contribute to the colonial economy soon proved difficult. Transportation over the Wallingford pathways was cumbersome and quite dangerous in certain times of the year, especially when attending religious services from their scattered farms. Because of this, the North Farmers petitioned to have a separate meetinghouse closer to their homes. In 1727, a structure was raised on Meeting House Hill, now the corner of Ann Street and Dryden Drive in Meriden, with its first burying ground set to the east near the summit of the hill. But it wasn't a simple decision or build.

Tradition has it that the location of the first meetinghouse was disputed and quarreled over incessantly. The farmers living near Pilgrim's Harbor (today's downtown district) wanted the meetinghouse to stand at the corner of present-day Curtis and Ann Streets, but those who lived farther east, just west of Black Pond, in an area called Dog's Misery wanted it at the site where it was finally built, Meeting House Hill. During the initial build, the lumber was taken to the western slope of Meeting House Hill to await the arrival of other materials needed for the structure. During the night, the Pilgrim's Harbor group, still hoping to have it built at the junction of Curtis and Ann Streets, teamed up and carried the lumber to their site. The next day, a bitter controversy followed, but the Dog's Misery residents won. The men who had hauled the lumber away in the night had to bring it back to Meeting House Hill during the daylight hours amid the jeers of the winners.

The first attempt at organization was made in 1728, when a petition to the General Legislature was granted and the region established as a village under the official name of Meriden, though still in part connected with Wallingford.

In the mid-eighteenth century, Hartford of the Connecticut Colony was also spilling southward in its parallel growth, similar to New Haven's northern climb. The arrival of English colonists in the seventeenth century had marked a turning point in the region's history. As the century progressed, the aforementioned Hooker led a fruitful and prosperous colony in and around Hartford. Of its people, Jonathan Gilbert, the colony's customs collector, marshal and a representative to the Connecticut legislation, in addition to being a saloon- and innkeeper, was granted the first land in present-day Meriden, according to the 1906 Curtis and Gillespie book *A Century of Meriden.* As early as August 28, 1661, Gilbert was granted "a farm to ye number of 300 acres of upland and 50 acres of meadows," where he immediately proceeded to develop in the northern section of the town. The reference also stated that on May 15, 1662, Gilbert was granted permission "to keep an ordinary, or inn, at his house at Cold Spring."

After Gilbert acquired his farm at Cold Spring, which he called Meriden, likely inspired by his birthplace, Meriden, near Birmingham,

This facsimile signature of Jonathan Gilbert, Meriden's first landowner, was taken from his will. *Author's collection.*

This circa 1690 structure, part of the original Belcher Farm, is considered the first area house of entertainment serving as a tavern and respite for travelers. *Meriden Historical Society.*

England, he put Edward Higby in charge of it. So far as can be learned, Higby was the first white man to take up residence in Meriden. Gilbert later built an inn on this same stretch. On October 15, 1664, Higby bought off of a Hartford Native American the land between the farm of Jonathan Gilbert and "Pilgrims Harbour."

Jonathan Gilbert never lived in the inn he built. As one of the earliest settlers in Hartford, Gilbert was by trade a saloon- and innkeeper, a position of great respectability at the time. He also engaged in the fur trade regularly with Boston, Massachusetts, and overseas. Conveniently, the locality of Gilbert's farm abounded with beavers and other fur-bearing animals (today's Beaver's Pond in Meriden), thus allowing for ample trapping. In fact, Gilbert built a warehouse on the river in Hartford from which he shipped furs taken from his farm in Meriden. These furs were carried on ships owned by his son-in-law, Andrew Belcher, who later, by purchase, became the owner of the Meriden farm, now known as the Belcher Farm. Coincidentally, to ensure that this steady flow of furs that the colonists procured would not be impeded by Native hostility, it was declared early on that this Hartford land was a neutral zone and all Native Americans could come and trade in peace as well.

In the 1600s and 1700s, Meriden—situated halfway between the Connecticut Colony on the north (Hartford-Wethersfield today) and the New Haven Colony on the south—became a stopping place for colonists who traveled by horse or by foot; the first wagon did not make its appearance until 1789. The Belcher Tavern, which was part of the farm, was one of the area's well-known resting places. In the eighteenth century, most travelers to Meriden came into or left the town either by the original Native American trail or "Country Road"—today's Colony Street—to the north; Wall Street, which was then called Westfield Road, to the east; Curtis Street to the south; or by present-day Johnson Avenue (as Main Street wasn't opened until 1812) to the west.

During this time, settlements began to creep into the western and southwestern parts of the present limits of Meriden. Many of these land deeds used the phrase "hoop ground land." Such land, though swampy, was then the most valuable in the town because it produced the material for making hoops. These hoops were in great demand in the West Indies, with which Meriden did consistent business.

As the presence of abundant water resources—courtesy of the Quinnipiac River and its tributaries—laid the groundwork for future industrial development, the latter half of the eighteenth century witnessed a gradual shift in Meriden's character. The arrival of skilled artisans, particularly blacksmiths and silversmiths, marked the beginnings of an emerging craft economy. These skilled individuals formed the foundation for the burgeoning silverware industry that would later define Meriden.

By the early nineteenth century, Meriden's population had grown significantly, fostering a growing desire for independence from Wallingford. Residents yearned for greater control over local affairs. In 1806, their aspirations materialized when the Connecticut General Assembly officially incorporated Meriden as a separate town. This marked a pivotal moment in the town's history, signifying its emergence as a distinct entity with a promising future.

The incorporation of Meriden coincided with a period of burgeoning industrial activity across the United States. Meriden, with its skilled workforce and abundant waterpower, was perfectly positioned to capitalize on this trend. The early nineteenth century witnessed the establishment of several key enterprises, including Samuel Yale's pewter factory in 1794 and Ashbil Griswold's Britannia ware factory in 1808. These pioneering ventures

This early Village of Meriden map details its town center before it would move westward, due to the area's establishment of the railroad line. *Author's collection.*

laid the groundwork for the silver industry that would propel Meriden to national prominence.

The early history of Meriden paints a portrait of a community in transformation. From its humble beginnings as a quiet, agricultural outpost to its emergence as a burgeoning industrial center, Meriden's journey reflects the broader changes sweeping across the young nation. The presence of Native Americans, the arrival of European settlers and the gradual shift toward industry all contributed to shaping Meriden's identity. This early period laid the foundation for the Silver City's future prosperity, paving the way for a rich industrial heritage that would leave a lasting mark on American history.

Before Meriden was a bustling town, let alone a city, it was a sparsely populated frontier, a part of the larger landscape of colonial Connecticut.

Its history, like that of many New England settlements, is intertwined with the narratives of Native American tribes, European colonization and the arduous journey from wilderness to community. The story of Meriden's early history is one of resilience, adaptation and a commitment to progress. From its humble beginnings as a farming community to its rise as a prominent industrial center, the city has consistently reinvented itself. Today, while the dominance of the silver industry has waned, Meriden's innovative spirit from its earliest days continues to drive its evolution into the present day.

2

Captain John Couch

Meriden's Most Revered and Celebrated Revolutionary War Hero

In the quiet town of Meriden, amid the echoes of history, lies the tale of an unsung hero whose bravery and leadership played a vital role in the quest for American independence. Captain John Couch, a name perhaps not as widely recognized as other Revolutionary War figures, nonetheless stands as a testament to the indomitable spirit of the early American patriots. His story is one of courage, sacrifice and unwavering commitment to the cause of freedom—a story that deserves to be remembered and celebrated for generations to come.

Captain John Couch was born on August 6, 1725, in Branford, Connecticut, a descendant of Simon Couch and Elizabeth Plant and ancestor to the multimillionaire Henry B. Plant, owner of the Plant system of railroads and steamboats of the South.

Couch had settled in Meriden around 1746 after purchasing a farm from Aaron Lyman in the present-day Wall and North Wall Street area. The following year, Couch married Azubah Andrews, a descendant of William Andrews, an English colonist who in 1635 built the first meetinghouse in New Haven and later married the daughter of William Gibbands, the colonial secretary of Connecticut in 1657.

John Couch and Azubah had two daughters: Sarah, who married Judge Jonathan Collins, a noted judge in New York State, and Elizabeth, who married Theophilus Hall Jr., son of Reverend Theophilus Hall Sr., Meriden's first minister.

The Couch family seemed to be militarily inclined. Samuel Couch, the son of Simon Couch, was a captain of militia in 1690 and the wealthiest and most influential man in Fairfield, Connecticut. Thomas Couch served in the American Revolution and was with General Richard Montgomery at the Siege of Quebec. Later, Major General James Nash Couch, a graduate of West Point, performed distinguished service in the late war. Captain John Couch's grandson John was born in Meriden in 1796. In later years, he, too, was captain of the Meriden militia, following the military precedents of the family: Samuel Couch was captain in 1695; John Couch was captain in 1695; and John Couch captain from 1774 to 1777.

When Paul Revere made his legendary ride on April 18, 1775, warning that the "British are coming," Connecticut could have been more prompt in responding to Massachusetts militarily. As it was, Connecticut was one day late in hearing "the shot heard round the world," which resounded from Lexington Green the following day on April 19, 1775. A postrider spread the word from Lexington to Norwich, Connecticut, the following day, and on the trip westward toward New Haven, news reached Wallingford on April 21.

The American Revolution had begun.

Captain John Couch and his company in Meriden were called out under an act of the General Assembly for the defense of the colony. Then the news of the Lexington Alarm hit; at one hour's notice, with eighteen men, four horses and one wagon, the group was assembled and marched north, briefly stopping at the local green on the southeast corner of Broad and East Main Streets today, before the trek toward Massachusetts. They were ferried across the Connecticut River at Hartford, rested on the Sabbath and then continued on their journey for the defense of Boston. However, before they could reach there, word had reached Couch and his men that they were not needed, so they turned back to come home to Meriden.

In the summer of 1776, following General George Washington's appointment as commander in chief of the Continental army in June 1775, Couch was commissioned as an officer and, along with his first and second lieutenants and eighty-six men, assigned for duty as a part of Colonel Philip Burr Bradley's battalion in Wadsworth's Brigade. The unit was stationed at Bergen Heights and Paulus Hook—strategic locations along the present-day waterfront of Jersey City, New Jersey—during the greater part of the summer and early fall, as part of the Continental army's defensive preparations against British advances.

That October, after engaging the enemy in both places, Couch's troops headed north to Fort Lee and the defense of Fort Washington. But as it turned out, the Battle of Fort Washington was the final devastating chapter in General Washington's disastrous New York campaign. It was there that the entire garrison was taken prisoner on November 16, 1776, including Couch with his first lieutenant and thirty-one men, including fellow Meridenites Steven Atwater, Benjamin Austin, Jonathan and Moses Hall, Gideon Ives, John Pierce and Gideon and Samuel Rice. John Couch was in a British prison on Long Island for quite some time after his capture. According to his Revolutionary War docket, there exist various receipts for money conveyed by the state to men in prison on Long Island in 1777. John Couch's name is among those signing. He evidently gained his freedom during the war, as he appears as captain of the Tenth Regiment, which was ordered to Peekskill in 1777.

On his return to Meriden, he was a man of high and forceful character and the owner of a substantial estate. With this influence, in 1786, Couch

This headstone of Captain John Couch, Meriden's most revered and celebrated Revolutionary War hero, is located in the city's Broad Street Cemetery. *Author's collection.*

was elected as one of a committee of three charged with requesting the Connecticut Assembly separate the town of Meriden from Wallingford.

After the death of his wife, Azubah, in 1799, Couch found solace in the companionship of Eunice Andrews Yale before marrying Sarah Moss in 1800, who would survive him by two years.

On April 11, 1806, Captain John Couch died in the neighboring town of Wallingford at the age of eighty. His legacy is preserved in the Broad Street Cemetery in Meriden, where he was laid to rest.

His contributions to the Revolutionary War were recognized by the Daughters of the American Revolution, who named him a DAR Patriot Ancestor. The Captain John Couch Branch No. 2 of the Connecticut Society of the Sons of the American Revolution is also named in his honor.

Captain John Couch's life story is a remarkable example of the courage and dedication exhibited by the early American patriots. His service to the Continental army and his unwavering commitment to the cause of independence are a tribute to his character and bravery. As we remember and honor the contributions of individuals like Captain Couch, we gain a deeper appreciation for the sacrifices made by those who fought for the freedoms we enjoy today.

3

CHATHAM FREEMAN

From Bondage to Freedom

Regardless of the underlying political and economic causes of the American Revolution, the patriotism of our country is what we seem to recall. The ideals of freedom and an end to repression have also always been seemingly identified with the Revolution, even for an enslaved man of color.

Private Chatham "Old Chat" Freeman was born about 1750 in Africa and brought to America by slave traders when he was a child or a young man. Upon his arrival, he was enslaved by Noah Yale of Wallingford, in a time before Meriden was incorporated as a town and still part of Wallingford.

He was probably known simply as "Chatham" before the war, with no last name. The unique given name may have likely referred to William Pitt, Earl of Chatham, the most important leader in Parliament during the French and Indian War. William Pitt was given the title Earl of Chatham in 1766, so perhaps Chatham, the enslaved man, was named then or sometime shortly thereafter.

Noah Yale was a Wallingford farmer. He and his wife, Anna, had ten children between 1745 and 1768—seven boys and three girls—but unfortunately three of the boys and one of the girls died before the start of the Revolution in 1775. The eldest surviving son, named Noah after his father, died the following year, in December 1776, while serving as soldier. He was only twenty-seven years old. At this time, his three surviving brothers were Thomas, aged twenty; Joel, aged seventeen; and Asahel, aged twelve.

Thomas had served in the Connecticut militia from August to December 1776 but returned home when his elder brother died.

When another round of the militia was called out in the spring of 1777, Noah Yale offered Chatham as a substitute for one of his sons, either Thomas or Joel, to spare the son from his obligated service. Under colonial Connecticut law, young white men were required to serve in the militia, but enslaved men like Chatham were not; however, their enslavers could offer them as substitutes. It can be assumed that the death of the younger Noah Yale in December 1776 shook the family and made Noah and Anna reluctant to have Thomas return to military service or to have Joel serve at all.

Noah Yale offered Freeman's emancipation in exchange for fighting as a substitute for his son. Chatham took this opportunity to obtain his freedom and enlisted on June 2, 1777. He served as a private in the Sixth Connecticut Regiment of the Continental army led by Major Eli Leavenworth until his discharge in 1780. This regiment consisted of mostly men from New Haven County, and Chatham surprisingly even found himself in the same company as an acquaintance, a fife player from Wallingford.

During Freeman's three years of service with the regiment, he found himself in some trying situations. He spent the summer of 1777 at Peekskill, New York, training on the banks of the Hudson River. He later spent that winter at West Point making fortifications around the area known as "Meigs Redoubt," named after Colonel Jonathan Meigs, and participating in conflicts along the riverside, including the Battle of Stony Point, where the Americans attacked an important British fort.

Freeman was honorably discharged from the army on April 25, 1780, and returned to Wallingford shortly thereafter in 1782. Freeman didn't receive his freedom right away though. Instead, Freeman and Yale revised their original deal. Chatham wanted to marry another Yale-owned slave, Maria, then known simply as "Rhea," who was ten years older than Chatham. Yale proposed that he would allow this if Freeman would work for him an additional seven years. Although this certainly prolonged Freeman's quest for freedom, he was determined to start a family with Rhea. Freeman agreed to Yale's offer and worked the extra time. Following their emancipation, the couple's marriage took place. Soon thereafter, Chatham and Rhea welcomed a son named Jube and then a daughter named Kate. It is probable that Chatham, like many free African Americans, used the last name "Freeman," probably from the time he was released from enslavement. It is unknown whether the name was given to him by the court or if he might have chosen this last name himself.

Slavery was commonplace: merchants, ministers, politicians, military officers, physicians, lawyers and farmers enslaved people. Statistics show that by the latter half of the eighteenth century, New London—a bustling seaport on Connecticut's coast—led the state in the number of white versus enslaved African and Black residents with a white population of 5,366 and a Black population of 522. New Haven had a white population of 5,224 and a Black population of 160, whereas, according to the 1762 population list, Wallingford, with a populace of just under 4,000, had 182 Black residents.

Chatham was a free man indeed. He had a family, a small house and even a little money. One incident would temporarily change all of that. During his middle years, someone asked Chatham to underwrite for him, to which he obliged. Thinking he was only a witness, "an evidence," as Chatham called it, he was conned. Unfortunately, the gentleman never made good on his transaction, leaving Chatham out.

"I was nossin but a nebula, massa. I was nossin of a nebula," Chatham noted.

The town pitied him, so far as one man gave him a silver watch to be raffled, which brought in thirty dollars. With some other help, Chatham Freeman was back on his feet and provided with a small house once again.

Affidavits in Chatham Freeman's pension file indicate that he was an African American of good standing. One such record, signed by a man named Samuel Paddock Jr., says that "I well know the above named Chatham Freeman that he is a free Negro man of good character." This statement is dated April 6, 1818, and at the bottom of the same document, Judge Simeon Baldwin wrote on August 21, 1818: "I certify that it appears to my satisfaction that the applicant Chatham Freeman is an old, infirm, poor negro man who needs the assistance of his Country for support."

Freeman was one of thousands of ordinary soldiers who helped win the Revolutionary War. Congress made promises to them—of land grants, bounties and routine pay—that it was slow to fulfill. As these veterans resumed their civilian lives with no help from the free governments they had fought to create, many struggled. For some, Congress and the public seemed indifferent to them. That started to change in the years following the War of 1812, as the generation that had fought and won the Revolutionary War began to grow old, including Freeman. To remedy this, Congress introduced Revolutionary War Pensions around 1800.

The freeman (voter) statute, under early state constitutions, allowed African American voting rights (as Chatham most likely did vote, although

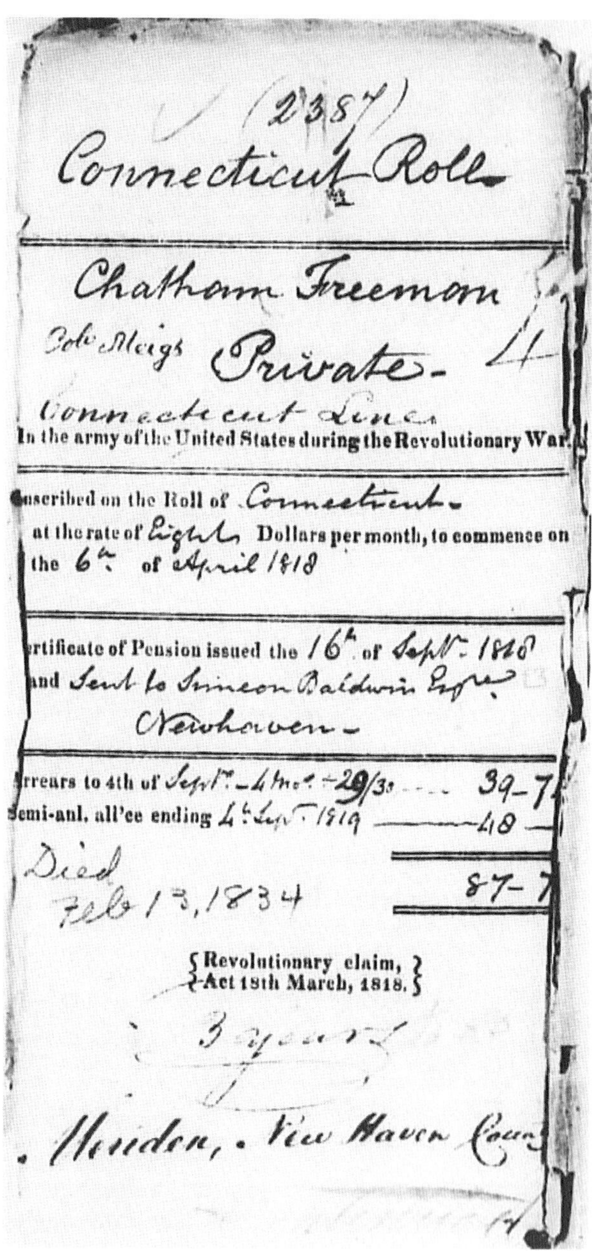
(2387)

Connecticut Roll

Chatham Freeman

Col. Meigs Private - 4

Connecticut Line

In the army of the United States during the Revolutionary War.

nscribed on the Roll of Connecticut

at the rate of Eight Dollars per month, to commence on

the 6th of April 1818

rtificate of Pension issued the 16th of Sept. 1818

and Sent to Simeon Baldwin Esqr.

Newhaven -

rrears to 4th of Sept. - 4 mos. 29/30 --- 39-7

emi-anl. all'ce ending 4th Sept. 1819 ---- 48 -

Died

Feb 13, 1834 87-7

Revolutionary claim,

Act 18th March, 1818.

3 years

Meriden, New Haven Coun

This photograph is of the cover page of Chatham Freeman's 1818 Revolutionary War Pension File today found in the National Archives. *Meriden Historical Society.*

Chatham Freeman fought in the Revolutionary War, and for that service, he was freed from slavery in 1782. To commemorate his life and service, a memorial was placed on the Broad Street median in 2008. *Meriden Public Library.*

voting records do not exist today). However, in 1814, African American voting rights were reversed by the Connecticut legislature inserting the word *white* into the statute. By 1818, a new state constitution had been adopted in Connecticut that outlined a race requirement for voters, thereby depriving African Americans of equal representation in the state's electoral process.

In 1818, at the age of sixty-eight, Freeman was able to prove he was poor and so received a pension under the Pension Act of 1818. Freeman received a pension of eight dollars a month, or ninety-six dollars a year; thus this yearly pension was worth twice as much as the net worth of his property.

According to the Pension File of Chatham Freeman, Revolutionary claim, Act 18th March 1818:

> *State of Connecticut—New Haven County I Chatham Freeman a resident citizen of the United States, of Meriden in said County and State aforesaid, do on oath declare that I served my country as a soldier on the Continental establishment for the period of three years, during the Revolutionary war—that on the 2nd day of June 1777 I enlisted as a private in Captain Leavenworth's Company, in the fourth Regiment Connecticut Line,*

> *commanded by Col Meigs, in which company and Regiment, I continued faithfully to serve during the period of my enlistment viz. three years, at the expiration of which I was honourably discharged. But by time & accident, my discharge is lost and cannot now be produced. I further declare on oath that by reason of extreme poverty, I now need the assistance of my country for support. I therefore pray that I may be placed on the pension list, pursuant to the Act of Congress passed March 18th 1818 Dated at New Haven April 6th 1818 Chatham* [X] *Freeman*

Two years before his death, in 1832, Congress had passed an act providing pensions to nearly all surviving soldiers of the Revolutionary War. Tens of thousands of men had qualified and received annual pension payments, and in the years that followed, Congress extended those benefits to the widows of Revolutionary War soldiers—first to women who were married to soldiers during the war and later to any widow whose husband had borne arms in the war, so long as she had not remarried.

Chatham lived and prospered in Meriden as a free Black man until his death on February 13, 1834. He was about eighty-four years old and is believed to be buried today in an unmarked grave in the Broad Street Cemetery. In May 2008, a memorial was placed on the Broad Street grass median to the east of the cemetery on Memorial Boulevard recognizing him.

The story of Chatham Freeman is not a tale of skin color. Instead, it is about equality. The Revolutionary War was not fought to perpetuate slavery, as was a later conflict; it was fought to establish American independence and create a nation dedicated to the proposition that all men are created equal—a proposition we continue to struggle to realize in our own time.

4
Hidden in the Hills

The Story of the Golden Parlour Mine

Connecticut is rightfully called the birthplace of American mining, as there are over six hundred abandoned mines within the borders of the state. In the precolonial days, Native Americans mined rock and mineral resources such as flint, iron oxide, clay, quartz, steatite and mica. Although today, at first glance, there are no signs evident of a once-working mine in Meriden, the hills on the western part of Walnut Grove Cemetery would tell a different tale; for they are the only remains of an ancient working mine known as the Golden Parlour Mine. Although its name evokes visions of opulence and hidden treasures, the reality is more intriguing than gold itself.

The ancient farms of Dr. William Hough, the second physician mentioned in Wallingford's records, and Timothy Roys were once located adjacent to each other along the old Country Road. This land extended westward to the river, encompassing present-day Old Colony Road and reaching toward the Quinnipiac River. As early as 1712, through farming, a copper mine was discovered between these two properties and brought to the attention of the Connecticut Colony. Although the General Court allocated shares of the mine's output to both Hough and Roys, this venture proved to be of little benefit, as the mines were constantly flooded with water as soon as they were opened.

According to Gillespie and Curtis in *A Century of Meriden*, this small mine was originally operated in a search for gold, rather than any other minerals. But as time told, the mine likely showed copper minerals, in addition to quartz and/or calcite gangue, common along faults in the Hartford Basin. No other specific minerals are recorded in the scant historical information about the mine. Below are some highlights of this old documentation:

> *On the hill in the western part of Walnut Grove cemetery are the remains of an ancient working known as Golden Parlor Mine. There are two adjoining shafts still to be seen which were extended to a depth of twelve or fifteen feet. From the shafts, galleries or drifts led to the west a good many feet. The farms of Dr. William Hough and Timothy Roys were adjoining and ran from the Country road to the river on the west. That of Timothy's was wholly west of Dr. Hough's and the common boundary was somewhere on the hill or crest where the mines were dug. The Hough farm and quite a portion of the Roys holdings were during the greater part of the last century in the possession of the Wood family, and the writer has been told by Norman S. Wood and his nephew, Charles H., that when they lived on the farm it was possible to penetrate quite a distance into the old drifts. In one of the shafts the present superintendent of the cemetery, Fred F. Bowen, found quite a nugget of copper and also the remains of one of the ancient iron hammers, probably used by the workmen in the olden days. It is not positive that the present shafts were those of the Golden Parlor mine on the Roys lease or were made by those who were digging for copper on the Hough farm. The mines were not far apart.*

For years, occasional deposits of trace minerals were found, thus reopening thoughts of uncovering treasure, until it was decided to reopen the mines for excavating. It was with Meriden's first deed for mining privileges, dated February 8, 1735, and on the property of Timothy Royce, that the Golden Parlour Mining Company was formed. Founded by Benjamin Royce, Arthur Rexford, Samuel Androus and others from nearby towns, the company reopened one of the two abandoned mines with the hopes of striking gold. However, the mine likely yielded copper minerals instead. After years of minimal success, this too was doomed to be a failure.

Historical accounts suggest that the company might have faced ruin after dispatching a shipload of copper from the mine to Great Britain. The vessel, perhaps heavily waterlogged, never reached its port, potentially leading to its downfall. A similar story is recounted about a mine in the Cheshire Parish, which also failed due to a comparable mishap.

A few years later, on November 29, 1754, Katharine Whittlesey, daughter of the distinguished Reverend Samuel Whittlesey of

Wallingford, bought out the heirs of Timothy Roys all rights to the mines and minerals that had formerly been leased to the Golden Parlor Mining Company. However, it is unclear what she did with the property afterward, as there are no records left.

The adjacent Hough property began to see action as well. Eighteen years after the mine's initial opening, Dr. William Hough's claim (who was then living in Haddam) was reopened. The farm was now the homestead of his son, William Hough Jr., the blacksmith. On March 21, 1755, the son mortgaged the farm to his father, and this clause occurs in the deed:

> *The condition of the above obligation is such that if the above William Hough shall allow his said father free liberty at the mines on the west end of his home lot to dig for ore as he shall see fit, and shall have liberty to cut timber for the use of the mines or digging drains or whatever shall be needful for carrying on the work, and shall have liberty to pass to said mines, on the south side of his home lot, from the highway, to the mines for carting.*

Nothing was ever found, and once again, it was closed.

For over a century afterward, small deposits of copper and other trace minerals continued to be discovered, but the area never yielded much. Dr. Hough's house was later bought by a gentleman named Norman Wood, and the homestead became known as the Norman Wood Place. Located on the left side of the Walnut Grove main entrance today, it was here that the home stood for over two hundred years. This house and farm would be bought by the Walnut Grove Cemetery Association in the 1870s.

This old house was attractive, often stopping people for a second glance. Around 1930, this home was under contract to be purchased by a New York family who was considering its removal to their home state. Due to its historical interest, Meriden declined the sale, and shortly thereafter, a local resident, Russell White, bought the old home.

White had also recently purchased a 1760 home in neighboring Yalesville. Piece by piece, White decided to dismantle the Hough home, being careful to have all pieces properly marked to ensure their being placed in their original position. This was all taken to the Yalesville home and stored under cover.

He recalled later that the former owner had told him many tales of the old copper mines. These stories were of paramount interest as he took the house apart. He learned of its discoveries and of one such mine shaft that had several galleries that ran off in different directions. White was given several relics found within the mines, such as an old pickaxe and a metal wedge. He later proudly displayed them in the home he had reassembled at a lot at the corner of Broad and Gale Streets in Meriden. The house still stands today.

As for the abandoned mine today, there are still many depressions, dumps and prospect pits in the wooded area between Walnut Grove Cemetery and New Hanover Avenue to its west. Most of the workings of a depression that may have been the shaft are now apparently filled. But the tale of the Golden Parlour Mine continues to be shrouded in mystery. Was it purely a copper mine, or did it also contain hidden golden riches? Were some of the extracted copper deposits sold to the colony or perhaps even to the motherland for use in currency or decoration? Did a shipment of ore from the Golden Parlour Mine destined for England actually vanish at sea? If so, could this tragedy have led to the disheartened owners abandoning the mine?

As we stand amid the remnants, we can almost hear the whispers of those long-gone miners. Their dreams, their labor and their hopes echo through time. The Golden Parlour Mine, though silent now, continues to weave its enigmatic tale—a story of human curiosity and the allure of hidden treasures.

5

Meriden's Presidential Visits

Impact and Legacy

Thirteen of our country's presidents have made their way to Meriden, with each of these notable visits underscoring the city's historical significance. From George Washington's ride to take command of the Continental army to Franklin Roosevelt's visit to a historic crowd during his quest for a second term in the White House, Meriden has witnessed pivotal moments in American history.

George Washington traveled through Meriden in June 1775 on his way to assume command of the Continental army in Cambridge, Massachusetts, and again in November 1789 on a presidential tour. The route he took through Meriden would have been on the old Country Road, present-day Colony and North Colony Streets, and he was most likely greeted with celebration, a sign that the residents approved of his work.

In the autumn of 1789, during a long recess of Congress, President George Washington embarked on a monthlong tour of the New England states of Connecticut, Massachusetts and New Hampshire. His goals were to connect with the people, gather information and promote the fledgling federal government. At that time, the Constitution had been in effect for only five months and was ratified by just eleven states, thus needing broader support. Washington's presence served as reassurance to the public that the federal government was dedicated to their welfare. Vermont and Maine were not yet states, and Rhode Island was purposefully bypassed on the trip, as it did not approve the Constitution until the following year, in 1790. Washington's tour of New England was part of a larger plan to visit all thirteen of the original colonies, a mission he completed during his Southern Tour in 1791.

Although George Washington's visits to Meriden may not have been grand affairs, their impact echoed far beyond the town's borders. His trips symbolized the unity of the young nation and the promise of a strong federal government. His commitment to understanding the nation's diverse landscape and engaging with its citizens set a precedent for future presidents.

Forty years after Washington's visit, Meriden would lay claim to not one, but two dignitaries who would later become president of the United States. This memorable occasion happened in Meriden in 1829, when General Andrew Jackson, the president of the United States, made his tour throughout New England. Traveling by carriage from New Haven to Hartford—and a decade short of the institution of the Hartford and New Haven Railroad line—Jackson stopped off uptown and gave an open-air public reception from the stone steps of the Center Congregational Church.

"President Andrew Jackson stood up in a barouche at the southeast corner of the building (Central Tavern)," relates Mrs. Frances A. (Faith) Breckenridge, in her *Recollections of a New England Town*. "He was bareheaded, held a soft felt hat in his hand, his hair stood up straight, as it is seen in his pictures."

He was greeted by quite a concourse of people. Introduced as the "hero of New Orleans" by General Walter Booth, a local Meriden banker, Jackson shook hands with a large number of prominent men, passing one by one in line. He had bright eyes, his gray hair stood straight up above his forehead and, as a venerable, brave-looking man, he appeared worthy of his high position.

After this patriotic reception, he and his honorable escorts, including Martin Van Buren, reentered their carriages and proceeded to Hartford.

The exact date of the eleventh president of the United States, James Knox Polk's visit to Meriden remains unknown, but it is known that his visit was unscheduled and spontaneous. William W. Ellsworth of Hartford, then governor of Connecticut, was well acquainted with Polk from their time serving together in Congress. Historical accounts suggest that as the president's special train passed the governor's train in Meriden, the two friends may have briefly met and clasped hands from their respective trains. Although Polk served as president from 1845 to 1849 and Ellsworth was governor from 1838 to 1842, making their terms nonoverlapping, it is plausible that Polk visited Meriden during his 1847 Northeast Tour, during which he visited several states, including Connecticut.

Abraham Lincoln came to Meriden twice, the first time in 1848 when he and Connecticut's Congressman Truman Smith campaigned throughout the state on behalf of Zachary Taylor, the Whig nominee for president. Lincoln returned for a tour of New England twelve years later as he sought the Republican nomination for the presidency. During that circuit, he spoke in Providence, Boston and five towns in New Hampshire, as well as New Haven, Hartford, Meriden, Norwich, New London and Bridgeport. Although no record of Abraham Lincoln's Meriden speech from March 7, 1860, exists today, it is known that he did repeat the antislavery message he declared in his Cooper Union speech and again in New Haven just prior to his Meriden visit.

Today, Meriden has the cold words of history on a plaque on the northwestern exterior wall of the Meriden City Hall commemorating Abraham Lincoln's speech eighty-eight years after it was given. The plaque, installed by the Sons of Union Veterans of the Civil War, was dedicated as a memorial on May 30, 1948, marking the occasion and the approximate spot where Lincoln spoke from the "Town House," as the present city hall was not the same structure, then reputed to be the largest public building in the state. The plaque was designed by local notable sculptor Louis Gudebrod.

President Ulysses Grant came to Meriden twice: once on the evening of June 17, 1869, and again on July 2, 1870. Little is known of his first visit; however, during his second visit, delegates from Meriden consisting of Mayor Isaac C. Lewis, former Mayor Charles Parker and Dr. E.W. Hatch went to New Haven on the nine o'clock car to ask if the president could make an unplanned stop in Meriden. Grant agreed, and the news was quickly telegraphed to Meriden. Anxious crowds began to form, and Chief Engineer Charles H. Warner got out one of the fire engines and sprinkled Colony Street as far as Fraryville in North Meriden, making the road cool and entirely free from dust. About 2:45 p.m., the presidential train was heard in the distance as the crowd began to congregate in front of the crossing on Main Street. The president appeared from the cars with the Meriden party and was received with three ringing cheers. The citizens swarmed around their distinguished visitor.

The *Meriden Daily Republican*, a controversial newspaper, described the Grant family as follows:

> *Almost every man in the car was dressed better than General Grant. Mrs. Grant is certainly not a beauty. She is plain, decidedly "cross-eyed", and yet the face is a good one. A kind motherly-disposition is indicated—a face*

that one could trust and one that suffering will not appeal to twice. She was dressed very neatly, yet quite plain. The daughter, a nice plain-looking miss of perhaps fifteen years has very intelligent features, is lady-like and does not put on no heirs [sic].

This Abraham Lincoln plaque adorns the northwestern face of the Meriden City Hall. It memorializes Lincoln's 1860 visit to Meriden in which he sought support for the Republican nomination for president. *Author's collection.*

All over the city, a good number of decorations lined the streets; the old Country Road—Colony Street—was dressed with flags and streamers all along the route, and the windows and balconies of the numerous residences were crowded with sightseers. The waving of handkerchiefs and utterances of welcome for the president resounded.

The State Reform School boys were drawn up in line and saluted the party as it passed. One of the boys even handed the president a bouquet. Upon the party's arrival in Fraryville, a large assembly greeted the president. He responded by lifting his hat several times to the vast multitude of people. On their exit, three tremendous cheers were given for General Grant and three more for Mayor Lewis. The train then proceeded direct to Hartford.

In the presidential campaign of 1880, the Republican candidates James A. Garfield and Chester A. Arthur became president and vice-president, respectively. Their visit to Meriden was brief and without much coverage. Fate intervened when President James A. Garfield was assassinated in July, the following year. Suddenly, Arthur found himself in the Oval Office, tasked with leading the nation during a critical period.

The twenty-third president of the United States, Benjamin Harrison, and members of his cabinet, along with their guests, arrived by train in Meriden on July 3, 1889. They were en route to Woodstock, Connecticut, where the presidential party members were to be guests of H.C. Bowen for Independence Day. Of the several dignitaries on board, U.S. Senator Orville H. Platt of Meriden was the only one who spoke to the great crowd who had gathered to greet the nation's chief executive.

The *Meriden Daily Journal* gave the following account of the event:

> *President Harrison and entourage arrived by special train from New York. The depot platform was jammed full of people and several stood in the rain on the neighboring sidewalk while the windows in all the buildings and shops near the depot were filled with persons anxious to see the nation's chief. About 12:40, the train, drawn by Engine No. 82, pulled into the depot. As soon as the train stopped, Senator Platt appeared on the platform of the President's car. As soon as President Harrison appeared, the crowd began cheering. The volume of sound did not suit the Senator and he called for united cheers and they were given heartily....The President, it was expected, would make a short speech, but he said not a word, nor did any of his party except Senator Platt. Immediately after presenting Governor Bulkley, the train pulled out of the depot. As it started, several climbed up*

on the bumper of the car to shake hands with the president, the first one being W.W. Myatt of the Britannia shop showroom.

"The whistles blew, the bells rang, the cannon boomed, and the people cheered until the very hills seemed to resound with the joy of the greeting," related the *Meriden Daily Journal* of August 22, 1902, the day the nation's chief executive, Theodore Roosevelt, visited Meriden.

Never before in the history of Meriden had it welcomed such a distinguished visitor with as much enthusiasm and patriotic fervor as it did when President Theodore Roosevelt came to town. Having assumed the presidency less than a year earlier after the tragic assassination of William McKinley, Roosevelt was a dynamic and captivating figure. Every man, woman and child in Meriden took to the streets to welcome him. The president himself was immensely pleased, repeatedly congratulating U.S. Senator Orville H. Platt on the good appearance of the city and its people. Roosevelt remarked that the residents were of an "intelligently looking class" and thought Meriden would be a wonderful place to live.

On August 22, 1902, President Theodore Roosevelt visited Meriden. In this photograph, the president doffs his top hat to the celebrating locals. *Allen Weathers.*

President Roosevelt was scheduled to visit Hartford on that crisp day, but at the urging of Senator Platt, he agreed to make a forty-five-minute side trip to Meriden and give a brief address before continuing to the state capital. His train arrived at the depot at 2:59 p.m., where he and his party were greeted by a reception committee consisting of Senator Platt, Mayor George S. Seeley, Postmaster Henry Dryhurst and other officials. They were then whisked away in carriages, escorted by the Connecticut National Guard.

The thousands who waited at the depot cheered enthusiastically, and the president responded with frequent doffs of his hat and a broad grin. Crowds lined the streets as Roosevelt's carriage departed the station on State Street. Along the route, he was greeted by veterans of the Civil War at the soldiers' monument near the town hall and by a group of children on the Methodist church lawn, to whom he rose and bowed slightly. A little girl ran up to his carriage and handed him a bouquet, receiving his heartfelt thanks. Throughout the main streets of Meriden, flags hung from nearly every window, and red, white and blue bunting adorned hundreds of buildings, stores and factories.

One thousand flags decorated the International Silver factories, and numerous pictures of the president were displayed. At the town hall, a twelve-by-twelve-foot display was suspended over the sidewalk, featuring a picture of Roosevelt surrounded by stuffed heads of elk and buffalo. Fire bells rang on the president's arrival, guns were fired and every factory in the city sounded its whistles and bells as a twenty-one-gun salute climaxed the celebration.

Before leaving, Roosevelt mounted the observation platform in the rear of his presidential train and delivered a short but effective address: "Fellow citizens, I am most pleased with your welcome and most glad to see your beautiful little city, and I thank you for your attention." Then, with a final wave of his hat, Theodore Roosevelt disappeared inside his car as the train chugged out of the Meriden station.

Eight years later, on September 19, 1910, President William Howard Taft passed through Meriden in a special car from New Haven. He was accompanied by Colonel Isaac Ullman and Charles P. Brookes, Republican national committeemen. Across the country, the president had been receiving congratulatory messages regarding his encounter with the "Big Stick" the day before his arrival. His refusal to consent to certain plans of Colonel Roosevelt marked the beginning of a new policy for Taft, demonstrating his determination to maintain his position within the party, even if it meant a declaration of war against Roosevelt. Taft was a classmate of Dr. Edward

Wier Smith, a Meriden doctor, during their time at Yale, and they remained close friends throughout their lives. Due to this friendship, Taft also visited Meriden in 1913 to address a Masonic gathering at the First Congregational Church. In 1917, soon after the United States entered World War I, the ex-president returned to the city to deliver a patriotic address.

Woodrow Wilson, the twenty-eighth president of the United States, who in his first term helped create the Federal Reserve banking system, visited Meriden in 1912. As the successful Democratic candidate for the presidency, Wilson campaigned at the railroad station, contesting against Republican William Howard Taft and the Bull Moose candidate, Theodore Roosevelt. Wilson won the election and served in office from 1913 to 1921, ultimately leading America through World War I.

On that warm July morning, Wilson arrived in Meriden by train and stepped confidently onto the platform at the station. His presence was met with cheers and applause as residents waved American flags and children held up hand-painted signs. Woodrow Wilson's brief sojourn in Meriden remains a testimony to the power of presidential presence. His words echoed through the streets, inspiring generations to come.

A five-mile route leading through the heart of the city the morning of October 22, 1936, was packed with men, women and children out to cheer President Franklin D. Roosevelt and his wife, Eleanor, as they passed through on his tour of the state while campaigning for his second term. Governor Wilbur Cross and Senator Francis T. Maloney were in the open car as the car reached from Meriden from Middletown. From Preston Avenue on the east to Hubbard Park on the west, Meriden residents and those from nearby towns lined both sides of the road waving their hands and yelling their greeting to the president. The visit was historic because it was by far the largest crowd ever to greet a national figure in Meriden. The crowd was estimated to be about twenty-five thousand. The day was a holiday. Factory management permitted employees to leave their benches to spend a half hour in the center of the city to cheer their president. The local public and parochial schools dismissed classes as well.

President Roosevelt paused at Crown Street Square and spoke into microphones provided by the *Meriden Record* to a crowd of approximately eight thousand crammed into the square. After being introduced by Mayor Stephen L. Smith, the president spoke the following:

> *Mr. Mayor and friends. I am glad to come back to Meriden. My good friend, Senator Frank Maloney tells me that I spoke at this very spot*

On the morning of October 22, 1936, Franklin Delano Roosevelt took a five-mile route leading through the heart of the city before heading to Waterbury. *Author's collection.*

> *when I was a candidate for Vice-President of the United States. Since that time, a great deal of water has gone over the dam. We experienced an era of frenzied finances and a few years of false prosperity, followed by a depression.*
>
> *That we are succeeding in returning prosperity to the country is indexed by the better purchasing power of our people. I am told Meriden is the greatest silverware center in the world and that orders are coming in pretty well. I thank you for the great welcome you have given me and I hope it won't be sixteen years before I come back.*

As the president finished, a great ovation resounded through the center of the city. Many local people shook his hand before the Secret Service moved in to hold the crowd back. The president got back in his car and rode west past Hubbard Park and on to Waterbury.

This particular visit to Meriden was his second of three he would make to the city, with each time in quest of public office. His first visit was in 1920, when as a candidate for vice president, he spoke in the Crown Street Square but was unsuccessful in the victory, and his third time was in 1940, when his unheralded visit resulted in a brief two-minute speech from the rear platform of the stopped railroad to a several-hundred-person gathering. Throughout all three visits, President Franklin Roosevelt always symbolized hope and determination.

President Truman, the thirty-third president of the United States, spent only a few minutes in Meriden on October 16, 1952, but it was an exciting few minutes for the twenty thousand citizens who witnessed the event. Truman, making a political swing on behalf of Democratic presidential candidate Adlai Stevenson, passed through the city in a whirlwind tour of many smaller Connecticut towns, including Wallingford, North Haven and Middletown. The crowd at Crown Street Square was just a fraction of those who greeted the popular chief executive. Crowds lined the streets leading to the square, where he received enthusiastic applause on Cook Avenue, followed by ovations on East Main and Broad Streets as he left the city for Middletown. Though it was a brief visit, Truman took ten minutes to deliver

President Harry S. Truman addresses a Meriden crowd estimated at twenty thousand in Crown Street Square on October 16, 1952. *From the* Record-Journal.

a crowd-pleasing speech to those assembled in the square. In his speech, he criticized the Republicans for their actions in Congress and their campaign tactics. He also urged the Meriden community to "vote their consciences on behalf of the welfare of the country." At the conclusion of his remarks, he stood on the podium, smiling broadly and chatting with those around him as the crowd roared and applauded for several minutes.

Following Truman's visit, twenty-four years passed before Jimmy Carter, the former governor of Georgia and Democratic presidential candidate, spent ninety minutes in Meriden on April 27, 1976. During several speaking stops, he discussed foreign policy and the other Democratic presidential candidates, accurately predicting that he would win the Pennsylvania primary. He spoke at city hall to a crowd of about 150 and at the Latin American Society, where he addressed the audience in Spanish, filtered through a southern accent. Carter's campaign was successful, as he eventually secured the Democratic nomination through a series of primary elections and caucuses. His win was the only Democratic victory in the six presidential elections between 1968 and 1988, and it also marked the first time since 1932 that an incumbent president was defeated in an election. Jimmy Carter's commitment to international diplomacy later earned him the Nobel Peace Prize in 2002.

In the annals of Meriden's history, the presence of thirteen presidents stands as an indication of the city's enduring significance. As Meriden has hosted leaders who shaped the nation, these visits not only left a lasting mark on the city but also symbolized the intersection of local pride and national politics. As we reflect on these historic moments, we recognize that Meriden's legacy extends beyond its silver craftsmanship and industrial prowess—it is a place where presidential footsteps echo through time, connecting past and present.

6

The Historic Saltbox at 424 West Main Street

The Andrews Homestead

The history of the Andrews line in America started with the arrival of William Andrews in Boston in 1635. A notably successful and skilled carpenter, he built many of New England's earliest buildings, including New Haven's first meetinghouse. But it was his great-grandson Moses Andrews who would be historically connected to present-day Meriden.

Born in 1734, Moses, too, was a carpenter, as well as a farmer, a physician and, unfortunately for historians, a Tory. Over time, because of his political and religious affiliations, the patriotic citizens of Meriden had very little to do with him and often excluded or ignored his presence.

The land at 424 West Main Street on which the traditional New England saltbox home stands was acquired by Moses's father, Samuel Andrews, in 1720. Here, the family operated a sawmill on a large tract of land near the brook at the lower end of today's Bradley Avenue. In fact, a present-day survey of the original farm would cover the area bounded by West Main Street, Cook Avenue and Harbor Brook, through to Allen Avenue.

It is said that prior to farming, Moses Andrews took up medicine and was spoken of as a prominent physician in the area. Regrettably though, due to his loyalty to King George III and partly due to early colonial laws—it was forbidden that anyone even allow a Tory to come into their home—his work as a physician was indeed limited.

This allegiance likely had other repercussions, too. Moses, being loyal to British rule, was quite unpopular with his neighbors. Likewise, the Episcopal Church, which was bound by its laws to pray for King George III, did not find favor in the community. Moses had become an object of suspicion and was placed under heavy bonds and forbidden to leave the family farm without special permission. In fact, he petitioned for permission to attend the Episcopal Church in Wallingford, but permission was denied. Instead, he was told that, according to the Fundamental Orders of the Connecticut Colony in 1639, he should attend the Congregational Church in the parish of Meriden. Andrews declined and decided to hold services in his own home. At first, the home's parlor was set up with wooden benches for the worshippers, but when the situation became critical during the Revolution, services began to be secretly held in the basement, with heavy drapery covering the windows to keep the proceedings from the knowledge of his neighbors.

Concerned, even his uncle, the Reverend Samuel Andrews, grew incredibly uncomfortable and left for Canada, as did many other loyalists of the time.

Built in 1760, the Moses Andrews homestead was used as the first St. Andrew's Church beginning in 1789. *Dan Murdzek of the St. Andrew's Episcopal Church.*

In the years that followed the war, optimism grew for Andrews as animosity toward him declined. On March 31, 1783, Moses Andrews, then fifty years old, married Lucy Little, thirty-eight, of New Haven, and in the following year, she gave birth to a son, Moses, and three years later, to a daughter, Lucy. During this time, the family continued to hold services in their home in which Moses Andrews acted as lay reader, until 1810. By then, the Andrewses' makeshift church had gained enough momentum that it quickly outgrew its space, and the need to relocate was imminent. This growth spawned a suitable land donation by Benjamin Curtis, and ultimately, this would allow for a forty-five-by-thirty-six-foot wooden-structured St. Andrew's Episcopal Church to be built in late 1810/early 1811 on the southeast corner of the old Broad and Olive Streets where the Broad Street Cemetery is located today. Andrews died the following winter.

Coincidentally, when the application was made to build a permanent parish around 1810, there were eleven names (including Moses Andrews) on the document declaring conformity to the Church of England. This original document would be later sealed in the cornerstone of the present-day St. Andrew's Episcopal Church on East Main Street.

But the story of the homestead's namesake, Moses Andrews, continues to fascinate. He was seventy-seven years old when he died on November 24, 1811, and in the terms of his will, he dictated the division of the family home into halves: one for his wife, Lucy, and one for his son, Moses, who died in 1860, and daughter, Lucy, who died in 1888, to share. Evidence suggests that soon after Andrews's death, a north–south dividing line was drawn, with both parties having common use of the great fireplace and Dutch ovens, but a reason for this division was never proven.

Moses's wife, Lucy, died at the age of eighty-six in 1832; no grandchildren were born to their branch of the family tree. The West Meriden house soon passed through in-laws to Almon Andrews, who lived in the house and operated a flour mill in town for many years. In fact, in 1864, the house was first used as a school for the lower grades of the West Main Street School and was known as the Almon Andrews School.

Nevertheless, the story of the Andrews Homestead doesn't end with the Andrews family. The last surviving member of the Andrews family later willed it to the City of Meriden. After this transaction, the property underwent periods of neglect, decay and rescue as it was again used as a schoolhouse, rented as apartments and finally served as a daycare center during the world wars, which benefitted many working mothers.

It had been acquired by the Meriden Board of Education and undergone a two-year Works Progress Administration project in 1933 and 1934. Afterward, it served as a kindergarten for the adjacent Benjamin Franklin School and as a colonial museum for the city. Additionally, the house was used as a meeting place for various organizations such as the Daughters of the American Revolution, a local camera club and the Meriden Historical Society. Throughout each of these transformations, the house bore witness to the daily lives of countless individuals, becoming a familiar landmark and a space of learning and community.

The school board then relinquished its control of the property, and there were no provisions made for the maintenance of the museum. The second rescue came in 1940 when a group of interested citizens formed the Andrews Homestead Committee to consider means of raising funds to maintain the historic house. Funds were raised, and during the following year, it was repaired, redecorated and furnished with a collection of antiques. The committee was elected to membership in the Meriden Historical Society, and as a result, the society gained custodianship of the building. Interest waned during the next ten years, and it wasn't until 1952 that interest began to flare again. Another major restoration took place in 1954 under the direction of the Meriden Historical Society, with monies coming from the Cuno Foundation after the society had signed a fifteen-year lease in 1952 with the City of Meriden.

As custodian of the building, the Meriden Historical Society continues the upkeep of the interior of the house, while the City of Meriden owns the land and maintains its exterior. The lease is now renewed every ten years.

The Andrews Homestead Museum, as it is known today, offers visitors a window into bygone eras. Exhibits showcase the evolution of Meriden's industries, from silver manufacturing to the production of everyday household items. The original furnishings—a mix of donations from local families and period pieces—create a sense of stepping back in time. The museum also delves into the history of the Andrews family and the significance of the house itself, educating visitors about its architectural style and its place in Meriden's narrative.

The Andrews Homestead is more than just a museum. It is a witness to the enduring spirit of a community. From a family home to a schoolhouse to a cherished historical landmark, the Andrews Homestead has witnessed and adapted to change. As Meriden continues to evolve, the Andrews Homestead stands as a vital link to its past, ensuring that the stories of its residents and the city itself are not forgotten.

Town of...

7

Ashbil Griswold

A Pewterer's Legacy in Meriden

Ashbil Griswold was the Father of Meriden silver-making.
—anonymous

Tinware was little known in New England in the mid-1700s. The small amount in use at the time was of English manufacture and quite hard to come by. It was only after the Revolution that the business of making tinware increased steadily, creating a demand for a better class of goods. This demand manifested into the introduction of pewter-holloware, and similar to tinware, it is one of the oldest industries in the country.

This specialized metalware business was brought to Meriden about the year 1808 by Ashbil Boardman Griswold, or Squire Griswold, as he was sometimes more commonly known. He moved to the Clarksville (later Fraryville) part of Meriden to the residence of James Frary in the north part of town. It would be there that he first met Frary's daughter, Lucy, whom he would later marry in 1810. Griswold commenced business in a small shop near this residence where he manufactured teapots and made other articles from block-tin.

Ashbil Griswold was born on April 4, 1784, in Rocky Hill (then Wethersfield), Connecticut. Prior to coming to Meriden, Griswold apprenticed for five years learning the trade of block-tin and other forms of metalwork from Captain Thomas Danforth of Rocky Hill. Griswold and future silversmiths like Luther Boardman, who later settled in Haddam, and

Charles and Hiram Yale, of neighboring Wallingford, manufactured their wares for peddling and barter. Some of these items consisted of pewter spoons, dishes, teapots and many other smaller pieces that could be easily cast in metal and are highly collectible in today's market.

Ashbil Griswold was one of the first makers of Britannia-ware in Meriden, having begun a local business in North Meriden in 1808. *Meriden Historical Society.*

Ashbil Griswold was a meticulous recordkeeper, as evident in an existing Griswold "Day Book." What he made, to whom he sold, the date and the prices he got for these products are clearly recorded within it. The earliest entries are dated November 7, 1807, and were likely sold to Baltimore customers. (This can be projected from his connection with Danforth, as he largely sold his products in the South.) The "Day Book," along with a half-dozen others that later followed, was uncovered in the former estate of his son-in-law, William W. Lyman, on Britannia Street. (Coincidentally, on the death of his first wife, Lucy, in 1835, he married Ann Hall Lyman, mother to William W. Lyman, who would become one of the founders of the Meriden Britannia Company.)

Griswold's pivotal decision in relocating to the burgeoning town of Meriden placed him at the forefront of a community on the cusp of industrial growth. He wasted no time in capitalizing on this opportunity. Upon establishing his own pewter shop, his early acceptance stemmed from a combination of factors. His training with Danforth instilled in him a commitment to quality craftsmanship. Meriden's location provided access to transportation routes and raw materials, and the growing Meriden population in the early nineteenth century created a steady demand for household goods. But it was Griswold's expertise, which was honed through years of apprenticeship, that ensured the quality of his products.

While pewter formed the bedrock of Griswold's business, his entrepreneurial spirit led him to explore other avenues. By the 1820s, he had begun producing more ornate porringers and mugs, diversifying his product line and catering to a wider range of customer needs. Furthermore, recognizing the growing popularity of Britannia-ware—a superior alternative to pewter—Griswold transitioned into its production by the 1840s. This adaptability allowed him to remain competitive in a constantly evolving market.

Griswold's influence extended beyond the realm of business. He played an active role in the development of Meriden. Apprenticeship records reveal that he trained several individuals in the art of metalworking, passing on his skills and contributing to the city's growing industrial workforce.

His merchandise was sold mainly by peddlers, who worked in the areas of New England and several points south. It seems that the output of such a small enterprise as Griswold's could not have been large; in 1830, records indicate that he employed not more than ten or twelve men.

Ashbil Griswold was a progressive individual. With incremental success, Griswold built a residence at 50 Griswold Street with an adjacent shop he occupied until 1842, upon his retirement from business. This shop was separated by a lovely garden, and since there was no visible running water adjacent to his area in the beginning, he must have used either hand or horsepower. It was later told that Griswold's power was furnished peculiarly by an old blind horse traveling around a beam connected with the floor above.

Griswold took Ira Couch, pewtersmith and former apprentice, into the business as a partner. Their sales were primarily in flatware, which gradually increased to include other types of Britannia-ware. Ultimately, though, their business relationship as Griswold & Couch lasted only twelve years before Couch's death in 1845.

Ashbil Griswold had become a leader in industry, an energetic businessman and a highly respected official in the community, too. In fact, Griswold was quite active outside of his business. He was one of the organizers of the first Meriden Bank, started in June 1833, leading as its first president for the next three years, before being active as a director for some time later. The bank was initially started as a state institution, and in July 1865, it was nationalized, the name changed to Meriden National Bank.

Griswold was one of the wardens of the Episcopal Church in the city, as well as Meriden's justice of the peace. In city hall, Griswold served in the town offices of town assessor and of treasurer. His keen approach to municipal matters escalated him to represent the town in the state legislature in 1831 and again in 1847.

Despite his successes, Griswold's later years coincided with a period of change within the metalworking industry. The rise of electroplating technology in the mid-nineteenth century posed a significant challenge to traditional methods of silver production. How it affected Griswold's business remained unclear, but it likely played a role in the decline of his pewter and Britannia-ware production. By 1845, Griswold had sold his metal-manufacturing equipment to James A. Frary and began to settle into full retirement.

With his Britannia-ware production behind him, Griswold stood in the background proudly watching the likes of his former students James A. Frary, Horace C. and Dennis C. Wilcox and William W. Lyman, in addition to Isaac Lewis and Lemuel Johnson Curtis. Recognizing the shift in popular taste from pewter to Britannia metal goods, these men founded the Meriden Britannia Company. In the years that followed, this younger generation of Griswold mentees continued in the pewter and block-tin industry.

Ashbil Griswold died on March 30, 1853, at the age of sixty-eight, never seeing the immense success of the Meriden Britannia Company. He is buried in East Cemetery in Meriden.

Griswold's life and work hold a significant place in Meriden's history. He stands as a pioneer, one of the first to recognize the city's potential for industrial growth. His expertise and entrepreneurial spirit laid the foundation for the city's transformation into the renowned "Silver City." Griswold's legacy extends beyond his own business ventures. He helped shape a skilled workforce and fostered a culture of metalworking excellence that reverberated for generations in Meriden. Griswold's import has transcended his own lifetime, as he established a family dynasty that has left an enduring mark on Meriden's industrial landscape.

8

Chronicles of Community

Exploring the History of South Meriden

To many, South Meriden is a happy, self-contained enclave with its own church, ballfields, volunteer fire department and even an airport. Unbeknownst to most, however, the area known today as South Meriden has had several names over the centuries. Originally known by the local Natives as Falls Plain and laid out in 1689, this area's name was changed in 1832 to Hanover—a name it kept for almost a century—and in 1922, Hanover and Meriden were consolidated and the village simply became known as South Meriden.

The desirability of South Meriden as a site for a village was noted in very early times. It was part of a second grant of land New Haven Colony purchased from the aforementioned Native Americans in 1638. Those who surveyed the tract reported a place of great natural beauty at the head of the plain where the traprock country begins—ideally suited for a village, there being land for grazing, hop pole lands and a river with a fall for power.

In 1666, four years before the actual settlement of neighboring Wallingford, the founders of that town also visited this location and made a similarly enthusiastic report. By the following year, the first grants of land in Falls Plain had been made. In 1694, real change came to the area. Local planters found it inconvenient to go to Wallingford to attend church and other formalized meetings, and because of this, they requested permission to annex themselves to a town nearer than Wallingford. As early as February 19, 1689, during a town meeting, Wallingford resolved that Falls Plain should be

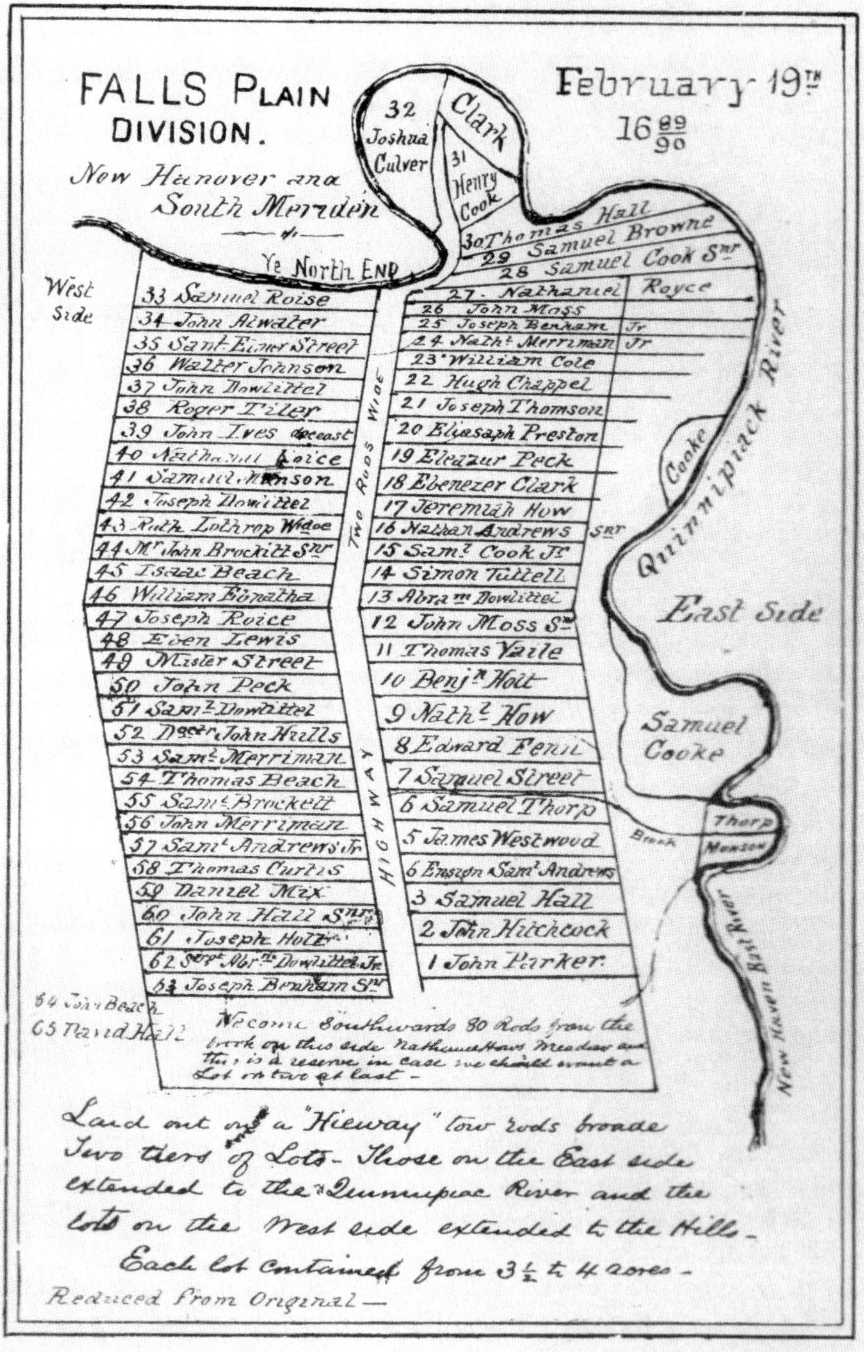

This early map of Falls Plain, later known as both Hanover and South Meriden, details the area's earliest landowners. *Author's collection.*

parceled out and a village built. For over a century, the village of Falls Plain would exist as its own community adjacent to Meriden.

Residents of the area were content with tending farmland, along with adequate hunting and fishing along the Quinnipiac River. But with the close of the American Revolution, the first growth of small industry began to emerge. Supplies and equipment that had previously been imported from the Mother Country were now being produced domestically.

Although the exact date of the first industry to locate in Falls Plain is impossible to determine, it was sometime during the late 1700s or early 1800s that a small factory on the Quinnipiac River was in action. It duly supplied waterpower to a number of other small waterway industries, among them Hough's Mill (farther west on the river), a pewter button factory and a wooden (and later bone) comb factory—a small firm that gave the area a moniker of "Boneville" for a short time.

In 1822, Julius Pratt began a comb factory in Falls Plain. It was situated on the east bank of the river near the lower end of Sheffield Street, present-day Hanover Road; however, the brook did not supply enough waterpower. (Pratt would later expand his factory upstream into Meriden to a point where Harbor Brook crosses Broad Street, near today's Brookside Park. Coincidentally, this area would later be known as the *Prattsville* area of town.) Under the direction of Pratt and his partner Fenner Bush, the business prospered.

Years later, in 1832, the water rights in central Falls Plain were purchased by Deacon N.C. Sanford & Company (later known as the Sanford, Parmalee & Company and also as the Hanover Company) and a new factory was built for the manufacture of augers. For most of the 1830s and the early 1840s, they continued the manufacture of augers, increasing to add skates and small goods of steel, giving employment to about fifty men.

Although the area of Falls Plain is deemed South Meriden today, the name of Hanover is ever-present in such designations as Hanover Pond and Hanover Elementary School and as in Hanover Street and Hanover Road. The name's derivation is quite peculiar. The name Hanover seemingly has two separate tales of origin. As most would agree that the two main resources for the history of Meriden are the 1870 Dr. Charles Henry Stanley Davis book *History of Wallingford and Meriden* and the Charles B. Gillespie and George Munson Curtis book *A Century of Meriden*, it is interesting to note that they differ on the origins of the selection of the name Hanover.

According to Davis, on April 23, 1832, as the local manufacturers broke ground for a new factory, it was collectively decided that, with Falls Plain on the upswing of attracting more residents and businesses, the center should have a proper name.

"Various names had been proposed for the village," wrote Davis, "and to decide upon one a special meeting of the company was called at the house of their agents. Four only of the members of the company were present at the meeting."

Davis continued about the name origin:

> *Various names were proposed and severally acted upon and rejected till the list was reduced to three. Neither of those could be adopted or rejected by the vote of the members present, and it was voted to come to a decision by casting lots and the first drawn to be the name decided upon. One of the members present was blindfolded. Another then wrote the ballots and placed them in a hat. The blindfolded man then drew out one ballot and handed it to another member who read the name Hanover written upon it. Such was the origin of the name, a name which Dr. Hough at the request of the agent of the company announced to the people who were assembled on the occasion of the boarding house, June 6, 1832.*

A Century of Meriden promotes a different origin of the name. Here, the authors imply that the name of Hanover may be drawn from the eighteenth-century copper mining industry on Milking Yard Hill, now part of Walnut Grove Cemetery. The name was adopted for the village of Falls Plain in 1832, but perhaps the name had an older pedigree. The men engaged in the copper-mining industry in the colony were mostly German, coming from Hanover, Prussia. Close to the mines on the eastern edge of the village were the smelting works—where the ore was crushed, refined and smelted. The locality was called Hanover due to the Germans who lived and worked there.

Since 1845, the Sanford property had passed into the conglomeration of two major American cutlery companies, the aforementioned Julius Pratt & Company of Meriden and G. & D.N. Ropes of Maine, now under the name of Pratt, Ropes, & Webb Company. Nearly seventy-five men were employed in this new venture, where they functioned under this name until January 10, 1855, when the company became the Meriden Cutlery Company. According to *A Century of Meriden*, the Meriden Cutlery Company was the earliest manufacturer of American cutlery, and its steel knives were the first successfully electroplated.

As a business, the Meriden Cutlery Company prospered greatly. Originally making ivory-handled knives and forks, the company gradually

The Meriden Cutlery Company began in 1855. It is said that the company was the first table-cutlery maker in the United States. The company was later bought by Landers, Frary & Clark of New Britain. *Author's collection.*

increased to other utensils until it embraced all table cutlery. Their supply came from all over the world: bounty steel and silver from the mines, pearl from the Indian Ocean, ebony from Madagascar, ivory from the African jungles and rubber and cocobolo wood from the Central American forests. However, by 1918, the Meriden Cutlery Company had been purchased by the Landers, Frary, & Clark Company of New Britain.

The village of Hanover was robust with activity and progress, but on October 22, 1861, Meriden heeded the call to host a Civil War training encampment, the temporary home of the First Regiment Connecticut Volunteer Cavalry. Located throughout the area of present-day Habershon Park, and along the southern shore of today's Hanover Pond, troops set up camp in a then "wide open, tireless meadow" known as Camp Tyler for what would be a period of three or four months. The Quinnipiac River had not been fully dammed yet. In fact, although it was considered a reliable water source, in truth it was a soft, rolling brook that wound through the vast pasture of meadow and wildflowers. Sodom and Harbor Brooks were mere trickles into this waterway then.

For 121 days, the lives of the soldiers of Camp Tyler were demanding and often monotonous. The primary focus was on transforming raw recruits into disciplined and efficient fighting forces. Beginning with a bugle wake-up call, inspections and physical exercises often followed. The bulk of the day was spent on drills, learning marching formations, weapon handling and basic combat tactics, while soldiers often spent considerable time practicing with their rifles, learning marksmanship and bayonet fighting.

After the start of 1862, however, the camp had made their final preparations to dismantle and remove into war; the aforementioned cutlery firm expanded, and the waterpower of the Quinnipiac River was further improved by the construction of a new dam. With this dam, water swiftly overtook the area of the Hanover fields, and a new lake, Hanover Lake, filled in the acres of flowing meadows.

If the village had an epicenter, it would have been the storefront of E.B. Clark, today's Tom's Place, on Main Street. Originally occupied by a Hensel Rice since 1864, the village store operated as the village general store, post office and meeting area. In 1882, when E.B. Clark bought the storefront, the residence also included the Odd Fellows Lodge. Tragedy hit on February 4, 1908, when the store was burned to the ground, including the Odd Fellow rooms above. The Clark store had to use a nearby makeshift building for the store and post office before being rebuilt.

The village's Main Street Methodist Church was organized as a society in 1851; however, meetings were held occasionally as early as 1839. After a few unique renovations over the years, it would be in 1914 that the church saw an immense overhaul. It was shingled, an annex was built and the stained-glass windows were put in. At the time, this church had a resident pastor and an average attendance of about seventeen.

Another church on the entrance of the village, the Catholic Holy Angels Church, was originally an offshoot of St. Rose's Parish of Meriden. This church was started in 1807 and built to accommodate members in Hanover, Yalesville and Tracy, Connecticut. It moved in the mid-twentieth century to a location on the South Meriden hill.

With the growth of the village, any such older arrangements for schooling would no longer suffice. Although Hanover School first appears in the Meriden town records in 1837, the exact building used could not be determined, though it predated 1844. In 1839, the school was also used as a Methodist Episcopal meetinghouse. It stood a little east of the present building and had but two rooms. When a new school was erected at a cost of $11,000 in 1868, the old one was removed to Cutlery Avenue. A

On February 4, 1908, the E.B. Clark general store burned to the ground. It is said that this fire was the impetus for creating the South Meriden Volunteer Fire Department. *Author's collection.*

two-room addition was made in 1905 when there were 163 pupils and 6 female teachers. In 1932, Hanover School—then called the Robert Morris School—burned down, but it was rebuilt in 1934.

Hanover Lake was a great source of ice for the residents of West Meriden. Between January and March during the early 1900s and into the 1920s, ice continued to be harvested in great quantity. Ice dealers such as the W.B. Johnson family and William Garlick could harvest upward of six thousand tons of ice in a good year. They would have cut and exported ice from these Hanover waters. In the pre-automobile and electronic era, the pond became a focal point for recreation for the city.

For ages, Red Bridge and the Quinnipiac Gorge have been a picturesque area of natural beauty. In 1881, the wooden Red Bridge, with its grand and heavy timbers, was built on Oregon Road. It was eighty-four feet long and would have cost $1,000 if contracted out, but instead, it was constructed by the town poor and one carpenter who was employed for fifteen days. However, this original Red Bridge was removed before 1912. Ironically, in those earlier years, Red Bridge was never even red. It inherited this nickname from an even earlier bridge that was a high-sided wooden structure assumed to be painted red. (Linseed oil was often added to help seal the wood to keep it from rotting. Rust was then added to the oil to keep fungi and moss from growing on the wood. This in turn tinted the oil red. Oftentimes barns and early buildings are still painted red from this tradition.)

The City of Meriden obtained Red Bridge in 1891 as part of a multiple-bridge purchase from the Berlin Iron Bridge Company, providing a link to what is now known as Oregon Road, the principal route between Meriden and the neighboring town of Cheshire. For years, Red Bridge remained a popular swimming hole. It had four small bathhouses for men and women, a lifeguard station, a diving pier and three diving boards mounted on the old bridge. In later years, it was revitalized multiple times, until around 1970,

Red Bridge today means quite the same as it did a century ago—an area to enjoy the natural beauty of the Quinnipiac River. *Meriden Historical Society.*

For nearly thirty years, Hanover Park, once regarded as Meriden's "Coney Island," was a celebrated and popular amusement resort. *Meriden Historical Society.*

when it was succeeded by a wider, studier, concrete bridge. Today, Red Bridge survives in close to its original condition.

Early in its history, the bridge was narrowly pardoned from destruction on August 11, 1887, as forty kegs of powder were used to blast in the ridge adjacent to the bridge, making headway for a railroad that was being introduced to the Hanover area of town. Rocks that weighed over a ton were thrown into the lake. One managed to go through the bridge; however, it was easily fixed.

Activity in this southwestern area of the city was enhanced by the opening of the Meriden and Waterbury Railroad in the spring of 1888. Although Horace C. Wilcox, Meriden's leading industrialist, passed away in 1890, his undertaking to create this central Connecticut railroad (one centered on driving down the high freight rates of the opposing Consolidated Railroad) was unveiled. The short line was never a success, but it left its mark on the topography of South Meriden. Trains stopped along Oregon Road to take on or discharge passengers near Chippie Island, where a wooden footbridge later provided access to Meriden's own amusement and recreational area, Hanover Park..

In 1894, the local trolley company opened the impressive Hanover Park on a thirty-acre tract on the northeast side of the lake. The park was readily accessible to the city's roughly twenty-five thousand residents and even to passengers on the Waterbury Railroad, which would stop to discharge passengers who could then walk to the park across a footbridge spanning the waterway.

Hanover Park offered a variety of pastimes and a great space in which to indulge them. It was a center of attraction. There was a merry-go-round with a double circle of animals, almost life-size, and a mechanical source of music, powered by steam in the center of the ring. Vaudeville acts, balloon ascensions and exhibits of various kinds were all weekly features found at the park. Baseball games were also played on the adjacent ballfield.

Hanover Park could have boasted about its boating facilities. The boathouse near the pavilion housed thirty-six rowboats and a launch in 1895. The sail around the lake and up the Quinnipiac River on this launch, the *Amelia*, was available at the price of one dime per passenger.

Although the exact closing date of the park has not been determined, it is likely that its demise occurred slowly throughout the 1930s, reflecting the rise of the automobile and improved roads, the movie house and changing tastes and competing interests. Trolley service ended in 1932 when buses

This photograph depicts the Hanover Lake boat dock with the Meriden Cutlery Company in the background. The sign at the end of the dock says, "The Launch Amelia Will Make Half Hour Trips Daily, Fare 10c." *Author's collection.*

Dossin Beach was a popular Meriden swimming resort during the 1930s. This image was taken on August 10, 1941, just prior to its closing due to unhealthy contaminants. *Meriden Historical Society.*

took over. In 1951, a large portion of the property was sold to the American Legion, and the balance was retained by the local transportation outfit as a bus garage.

For years, the area of Red Bridge on the west end of Hanover Pond was abandoned. It wouldn't be until the Depression years that Meriden rediscovered the area and began revitalizing the bridge and westward front, which was previously only wasteland. In 1932, Meriden acquired about one thousand feet of frontage of the north shore of Hanover Pond at its west end to develop a suitable recreational waterfront. To accomplish this task, Meriden had to draw off the lake, remove the undergrowth and embankments and fortify it with fine beach sand. By 1933, this project—which was originally called the Red Bridge Recreational Project—had been renamed Dossin Beach. It was also augmented by a new enlarged brick bathing pavilion for public use. The beach was named after the late Oscar Dossin, a gentleman who served Meriden for many years as a recreation commissioner. In the early 1940s, water tests revealed impure levels, and swimming was forbidden. It was also determined that pollution in the Quinnipiac and currents originating from Harbor Brook created an unacceptable health exposure, which forced the closure of the facility.

In 1922, Meriden and South Meriden were consolidated, and the village continues to exist as a vibrant and diverse neighborhood within Meriden. The remnants of its industrial past are evident in the converted factory buildings and the continued presence of skilled metalworkers in the community. Residents enjoy a mix of single-family homes and apartment buildings, offering a variety of housing options. The story of South Meriden is far from over. Initiatives focused on historic preservation, attracting new businesses and fostering a sense of community spirit will shape the neighborhood's future.

9

Slavery, Abolition and the Meriden Riot of 1837

A Journey Through Connecticut's Struggle for Freedom

Slavery is as old as America.

A Dutch trader brought the first slaves, likely white and of European descent, to America during the seventeenth century, and the institution of slavery spread throughout the colonies in the following years. Enslaved people arrived in the Connecticut Colony in the 1630s, but it wasn't until 1650 that in-state slavery was formally legalized. Although the North would later be considered the cradle of the antislavery and abolition movements, its early participation in slavery cannot be denied. There were a number of slaves in Wallingford and present-day Meriden who labored on farms and within families. These slaves were thought to be brought directly from Africa or even the West Indies, with which a brisk commerce was carried on by the people of central Connecticut.

The notion that all slaves were of African descent alone is entirely false. Those held in bondage were of African, Native American or even of the aforementioned white European ancestry. In fact, the first enslaved Black person didn't arrive in the colony until about 1680, when an initial thirty slaves arrived from Barbados. Later, about 1715, as the settlement of Meriden was seeing promise and growth, the importation of Native American slaves ceased. They were deemed hostile, specifically the shipments from the Carolinas, and unfit to commit to area families.

Colonial slavery developed within a world that was accustomed to unfree labor. Unlike the South's reliance on large-scale plantation agriculture,

Connecticut's enslaved population performed diverse tasks. They worked on farms, in shipbuilding, in domestic service and in skilled trades. By the American Revolution, Connecticut had the most enslaved people in New England, highlighting the economic integration of slavery into the colony's way of life.

The ideals and encouragement of liberty during the Revolution sparked debates about slavery. Connecticut's response, however, was a compromise, as seen in its acceptance of the Gradual Abolition Act of 1784. This law, rather than immediate emancipation, declared that children born into slavery after March 1784 would be freed on reaching adulthood (ages twenty-five for men and twenty-one for women). This approach, while a step toward abolition, ensured a slow decline in the state's enslaved population and protected the property rights of slaveholders. A 1797 amendment to this act later reduced the age to twenty-one.

Just as the Revolution spawned the United States of America, a principle emerged out of a revolutionary idea that forefather Thomas Jefferson expressed eloquently in his Declaration of Independence: "All men are created equal and are entitled to life, liberty, and the pursuit of happiness." How could a nation so constituted and dedicated to the proposition that all men are created equal enslave other human beings? This contradiction would eventually split the country in two a few decades later.

As the eighteenth century drew to a close, the African American population in central Connecticut held steady. However, by the early 1800s nearly 80 percent of those enslaved were free. This transformation may be due to the American Revolution, during which many northern enslaved people gained their freedom by running away; by fighting for the British or the Americans, which may have promised freedom in exchange for their service; or through the aforementioned state's gradual abolition law. Blacks were slowly gaining an economic foothold in the state, continuing to raise fears of Black advancement among white Connecticut freemen.

In 1837, there were about one hundred slaves in Meriden, and most residents viewed slaveholding as a mere disturbance rather than the national issue it would become years later. The Civil War was still twenty-five years in the future.

In 1837 and 1841, the agitation over the slave trade was at its height in America. Great bitterness was manifested, and the term *abolitionist* was in question. Mob law and aggression were rampant all over the nation, and communities were divided as party politics and personal ambition intensified the violence of political contest. This atmosphere was apparent in Meriden as well.

An uptick in the antislavery movement was seen, and a society of abolitionists composed a document that outlined the history and position of the Meriden antislavery movement.

Over 160 years later, during the winter of 1981, in a local resident's attic on Maple Street, the preamble and constitution of said document were found. This yellowed and stained paper relic also contained the names of the 118 original members of the antislavery group. Among the names of these founders were Fenner Bush and Julius Pratt, as well as Walter Webb, Harlow Isbell, Zena Murdock, Homer Curtiss, Major Elisa A. Cowles, their wives and several others.

The preamble and constitution of the Meriden Anti-Slavery Society read as follows:

> *Whereas we believe that slavery is a violation of the inalienable rights which are the natural possession of every man, contrary to the principle of Christianity, dangerous to the liberties of the country, and ought to be immediately abolished—and whereas we believe that we not only have a legal and a just right to utter our sentiments, disseminate our principle upon, and discuss the subject, but are under the highest obligation as moral beings to seek its removal by all honest, prudent and lawful means—and whereas we believe that the free people of color are unrighteously oppressed and stand in need of our sympathy and benevolent regard, we therefore, recognizing the inspired declaration that "God hath made of one blood all nations of men to dwell on all the face of the earth," and in obedience of our Savior's Golden Rule, "All things, therefore, whatsoever ye would that men should do unto you, do ye even so to them," agree to form ourselves into a society to be governed by the following:*
>
> *Constitution*
>
> *Art. 1—This society shall be called the Meriden Anti-Slavery Society, and shall be auxiliary to the American Anti-Slavery Society.*
>
> *Art. 2—The object of this society shall be to aid in the great work of effecting by all lawful moral and religious means the entire Abolition of slavery in the United States—the intellectual and moral improvement of*

Preamble and constitution of the Meriden Anti Slavery Society

Whereas we believe that Slavery is a violation of the inalienable rights which are the natural possession of every man, contrary to the principles of Christianity, dangerous to the Liberties of the country, and ought to be immediately abolished — and whereas we believe that we have not only a legal and just right to utter our sentiments, disseminate our principles upon, and freely discuss the subject but are under the highest obligation as moral beings to seek its removal by all honest, prudent and lawful means and whereas we believe that the free people of color are unrighteously oppressed, and stand in need of our sympathy and benevolent regard, we therefore, recognizing the inspired declaration that, "God hath made of one blood all nations of men to dwell on all the face of the earth", and in obedience of our Saviour's golden rule, "All things, therefore, whatsoever ye would that men should do to you, do ye even so to them", agree to form ourselves into a society to be governed by the following

Constitution

Art 1 This society shall be called the Meriden Anti Slavery Society, and shall be auxiliary to the American Anti Slavery Society.

Art 2 The objects of this society shall be to aid in the great work of effecting, by all lawful moral, and religious means, the entire abolition of slavery in the United States — the intellectual and moral improvement of the free people of color, and the correction of public opinion in regard to their situation, rights and privileges.

Art 3 The officers of this society shall be a President, Vice President, Secretary & Treasurer — with Five Directors who shall constitute an Executive Committee to manage the business of the society.

Art 4 The annual meeting of the society shall be on the fourth day of July, each year, or as near as may be to this time.

Special meetings may be called at any time by the Executive Com

Art 5 This constitution may be altered or amended at any regular meeting of the Society, by a vote of two thirds of the members present — provided said alteration or amendment shall be proposed in writing at a previous meeting.

During the winter of 1981, this circa 1836 preamble and constitution of the Meriden Anti-Slavery Society was found in a Maple Street home's attic. *Meriden Historical Society.*

> *the free people of color—and the correction of public opinion in regard to their situation, rights and privileges.*

Other articles in the constitution set forth that the society should have a president, vice president, secretary and treasurer and five directors, and that the annual meeting of the society should be held on July 4 of each year. Today, this document is in the possession of the Meriden Historical Society.

Despite the gradual emancipation law, the early nineteenth century saw a rise in abolitionist sentiment. National figures like William Lloyd Garrison and Frederick Douglass inspired local activism. Connecticut witnessed the formation of antislavery societies and the circulation of abolitionist publications. However, these efforts faced fierce opposition. Proslavery residents feared economic disruption and social unrest if slavery were abolished. This entrenched resistance culminated in the infamous Meriden Riot of 1837.

Upon the formation of this antislavery society in Meriden, a few of the founders, notably Levi Yale and the aforementioned Bush and Pratt, desiring that more be done in agitation of this great moral question, procured the use of the basement of the present Center Congregational Church and proposed a lecture by the Reverend Henry Ludlow, an abolitionist minister from New York City, on the evils of slavery.

On April 15, 1837, the lecture was announced from the pulpit of the church, and a test was made whether free speech could be maintained in Meriden. This proposal was met with adamant opposition from many citizens, including Judge James S. Brooks, a prominent and influential official of Meriden. Despite the opposition, the sponsors of the lecture insisted that the lecture proceed. This decision led to a confrontation between the supporters and opponents of the lecture.

On the day of the lecture, the meeting room in the basement of the church was nearly full when Ludlow began his talk. However, rumors of trouble brewing outside led to the door of the meeting room being locked and benches placed against it. The crowd outside, composed of local sympathizers and others brought in from Wallingford, Southington and Berlin, attempted to disrupt the lecture.

The crowd outside threw stones against the door to no effect. Eventually, two men carried a log from a nearby woodpile and used it to batter down the door. As soon as the door was opened, several of those from the lecture audience were assaulted with eggs and other projectiles. Although no one was killed, several were severely beaten.

The Meriden Riot marked a turning point in the fight for abolition in Connecticut. While the immediate outcome was a setback for the antislavery movement, it also brought national attention to the issue. The national press condemned the violence, and prominent abolitionists used the event to rally public opinion. Though slavery continued in the state for another decade, the Meriden Riot served as a stark reminder of the struggle for racial equality that lay ahead.

For the following three years after the incident, the church was without a pastor; however, in 1841, it procured the services of the Reverend George W. Perkins, a man of whom it is said "no mobs could control and violence silence." If the proslavery sympathizers in the church thought that here was a man who would be silent on the burning question of the day, they were entirely mistaken. Perkins apparently loved danger and boldly and persistently championed the cause of freedom for the enslaved. It is said that even his fellow ministers were tired of hearing him on the subject. Nevertheless, they respected his great ability.

As a catalyst for change, Reverend Perkins was invited to speak at Yale College on the subject of sanctification, into which it was presumed no pleas for the slave could possibly be brought. But when he began his address, he said, to the utter astonishment of his bearers, "Brethen, the greatest obstacle to Sanctification in the Church of America is slavery."

His work transcended the reaches of the church. Reverend Perkins was one of Meriden's foremost conductors of the local branch of the Underground Railroad. He risked personal injury and arrest through his efforts guiding the former enslaved from Meriden to stops farther north, such as Middletown and Hartford.

Perhaps no better example of the local sentiment against slavery can be that of a meeting held in the old town hall a few months prior to the war. The aforementioned antislavery spokesperson and local manufacturer of ivory combs Fenner Bush, among other remarks, said, "If the people of the south do not want to buy our combs, then they can go lousy. I believe slavery should be abolished."

In 1848, the state legislature officially abolished slavery in Connecticut and decreed for the first time that no person should be held in slavery in the state, an act that continued to provoke much debate. Even in the pre–Civil War climate, the church, under the direction of Perkins, voted to deny communion to any of the local slaveowners of Meriden.

Preceding the war, the 1850s were years of tremendous growth and prosperity. After the 1848 act officially ended slavery in Connecticut, the

Reverend George Perkins spent fourteen years as the pastor of the First Congregational Church in Meriden. In addition, he was an abolitionist who was active in the Underground Railroad. *Author's collection.*

experience of enslaved individuals during this period was complex, shaped by both legal changes and the realities of their daily lives. Former slaves gained legal recognition as free persons, allowing them to move, work and live independently; however, they had to adapt to a society that had long marginalized them. Some struggled to find employment, housing and education. Discrimination persisted, albeit in different forms, as the legacy of slavery persisted. Former slaves continued to carry the trauma and memories of their past, and as the struggle for full equality continued, challenges such as voting rights, segregation and economic disparities now came into focus.

Although the local history with slavery is a tangled web of economic dependence, ethical compromises and, ultimately, a substantial antislavery movement, Meriden still stands as a witness to the fierce resistance abolitionism encountered. Yet it also served as a catalyst for further action, paving the way for the eventual end of slavery in Connecticut in 1848.

10

The Underground Railroad in Meriden

A Haven on the Road North

The Underground Railroad, a clandestine network of safe houses and routes, today stands as a testimony to the courage and resilience of those seeking freedom from the bondage of slavery. While often romanticized as a literal subterranean railway, it was, in reality, a complex system of human compassion and defiance.

The town of Meriden emerged as a significant stop on the path to freedom as it was ideally positioned and central to the state to serve as a transit point for fugitives traveling northward. With the city's proximity to major transportation routes coupled with its growing industrial base, the Underground Railroad created opportunities for both employment and concealment.

As for Connecticut, it was the second colony after Massachusetts to pass a law recognizing slavery in 1650; ironically, it was the last state in New England to free its slaves. The state's position in the North belied its deep-rooted involvement in the institution of slavery. The nation grappled with the moral implications of slavery in the nineteenth century as a growing abolitionist movement was beginning to take root in the state.

After the Revolution, due to the efforts of missionary societies, the conscience of New Englanders was stirred. In 1833, an antislavery society was formed in New Haven, followed by one in Meriden. Some wanted to free slaves and send them back to Africa. This movement, fueled by religious and humanitarian principles, provided a fertile ground for the Underground Railroad to flourish.

As evidence of antislavery sentiment in Meriden, newspapers like the *Meriden Literary Recorder* published articles critical of slavery, and local residents participated in national antislavery movements. This supportive environment would have been essential for the Underground Railroad to function.

The Underground Railroad was a sophisticated secret system for helping fugitive enslaved people make it successfully to the North. This system was a geographical network of houses, churches, sheds and barns that may have held secret rooms called depots or safe houses; these were spaces owned by courageous landowners and operated by equally brave conductors who guided slaves from one station to another. Traveling primarily at night, many of the fugitives relied on rumors of safe houses and the guidance of the North Star for safety.

The state's geographic location was advantageous for those seeking escape along the Underground Railroad. Bordering New York and Massachusetts, Connecticut served as a crucial transit point for fugitives making their way to freedom in Canada. Major cities like New Haven and Hartford became hubs of abolitionist activity, with networks of safe houses and conductors facilitating the journey northward. While the state's role in the Underground Railroad is well-documented, the specific contributions of smaller towns and cities, such as Meriden, often remain overshadowed.

Passengers traveling the railroad often came to Meriden by an indirect route through Connecticut from New Haven to rural North Guilford. They were then likely transported to a way station in the Kensington section of neighboring Berlin, where they continued through to New Britain and Farmington. It was in Farmington that the Meriden line joined the less traveled Southington route and continued on to either Springfield or Boston in Massachusetts or up the Connecticut River into northern New England and Canada.

Routes were virtually everywhere and all leading north, but not all were destined for Canada. Some fugitives opted for densely populated cities such as New York and Philadelphia, whereas most simply yearned for freedom and continued into the new country. Along the way was Meriden, a popular route among the slave runaways. Many of the houses that once concealed these people remain today.

The town's antislavery society helped freedom seekers, and among these abolitionists were Meriden residents who were vocal about slavery. One such figure who stands out in Meriden's Underground Railroad narrative is Reverend George W. Perkins. A prominent abolitionist and minister, Perkins is believed to have harbored fugitives in his barn and attic. His connections to other abolitionists in the region likely facilitated the safe passage of those seeking freedom. While specific details about Perkins's involvement remain elusive, his reputation as a champion of human rights suggests his active participation in the Underground Railroad.

Unbeknownst to many local residents, the northeastern corner of Meriden laid claim to a stately number of safe-passage houses. Since these were found on the spur of the railroad line and adjacent to the frequented waterway associated with the "underground" passage, conductors utilized these routes to advance the runaways. More often, these homes were set on hills and possessed signal lights in a cupola or upper window. In one particular "underground" home on today's Westfield Road, it is said that a lit candle in the window of this early-nineteenth-century house meant that the coast was clear and that runaway slaves could find temporary refuge on their flight from the South.

Another of these safe-passage homes was the residence of Levi Yale. Yale had fought in the War of 1812 and had quite pronounced views against slavery. The oldest of several children whose father died early, he was running his mother's farm by the time he was thirteen. At the age of sixteen, Yale was the foremost supporter of his family by teaching in the winter and farming in the summer. Yale's hospitality at his farmhouse was gracious and always in good faith. He later became a civic leader in the town as first selectman and a member of the state's General Assembly.

The Milo Hotchkiss way station in Kensington, a neighboring town, further highlights the interconnectedness of the region's antislavery network. This station served as a crucial link between Meriden and other points north, underscoring the importance of cooperation and communication among abolitionists.

In *A Century of Meriden*, historian George M. Curtis described an occasion when Homer Curtiss and Harlowe Isbell hid fugitives in their West Meriden lock shop, which, in an act of proslavery arson, was later burned down:

> *At one time two colored men named Eldridge and Jones came north as jockeys and grooms to the two famous horses Phantom and Fashion. On reaching Philadelphia, these men were told by the Quakers that they were free under the law. They accordingly escaped from their masters and made their way to Meriden, and Mr. Curtiss gave them employment in his lock*

This was the homestead of Levi Yale, a Meriden man of pronounced views against slavery and a civic leader. It was used as a stop on the Underground Railroad. *Meriden Historical Society.*

shop. Their owners later ascertained that the ex-slaves were in Meriden and wrote to the sheriff offering him a reward if he would kidnap and return them. The sheriff took the letter to Rev. Mr. Perkins who wrote them that under no circumstances would they be allowed to regain possession of the men. Soon after, one of the owners appeared in person and demanded of Mr. Curtiss that he give up the men, and blustering and threatening the intervention of the U.S. government. Mr. Curtiss was not frightened and ordered the man from his premises. No further effort was made to take the runaways but for a long time they were very timid and scarcely dared to go on the streets. They lived here many years. Mr. Isbell was so carried away by the abolition movement that he removed to Kansas to assist in the attempt to make it a free state.

The Fugitive Slave Act or Fugitive Slave Law was passed by the Thirty-First United States Congress on September 18, 1850, as part of the Compromise of 1850 between Southern interests in slavery and Northern Free-Soilers. The act was one of the most controversial elements of the 1850 compromise and heightened Northern fears of a slave power conspiracy. It required that all escaped slaves, if captured, be returned to the enslaver and that officials and citizens of free states had to cooperate. The act contributed to the growing polarization of the country over the issue of slavery and was one of the factors that led to the American Civil War. According to this law, a fugitive could be seized without a warrant and a person found to be hiding a slave could be brought before a commissioner and fined up to $1,000 and six months in prison.

Connecticut, as with other free states, wanted to disregard the Fugitive Slave Act. Some of these jurisdictions passed personal liberty laws, mandating a jury trial before alleged fugitive slaves could be moved, whereas others forbade the use of local jails or the assistance of state officials in arresting or returning alleged fugitive slaves. In some cases, juries refused to convict individuals who had been indicted under the federal law. Meriden residents, in general, disregarded the act.

The passage along the Underground Railroad was novel in the sense that one had to keep steadfast while being also secretive in nature. Code words were used in defining the routes, such as referring to freedom-seekers as "passengers" and the people who guided them on their journey as "conductors." Also, passengers were referred to as "baggage," "bundles of wood," "cargo" and "parcels" and traveled between safe houses on the route known as "stations," which were owned by "station masters." Others who assisted passengers on their way north were known as "agents."

In pre–Civil War America, having any involvement with the Underground Railroad was risky, but for the freedom-seekers escaping enslavement in the South and the conductors who guided them, every step of the journey was dangerous, yet meaningful. Unfortunately, the guarded nature of the Underground Railroad has made it challenging to piece together a comprehensive picture of its activities in Meriden. Many records were destroyed or lost, and oral histories have faded with time. Historically, the Underground Railroad peaked between the 1830s and 1865, the end of the Civil War, and reached as far as Canada and the Caribbean. It enabled approximately one thousand slaves to freedom each year. Regrettably, thousands more tried and failed in their attempts.

II

From Pewter to Plate

A History of Silver Production in Meriden

Upon the products of her factories rests the world-wide fame of The Silver City.
—*anonymous*

During the first half of the nineteenth century, Meriden made its mark with two highly successful industries: tinware and the ivory comb business. But when these industries began to decline, the enterprise that gave Meriden the "Silver City" identity grew naturally out of the small but well-paying trade in Britannia-metal.

The earliest records of this industry start with Ashbil Griswold, who in 1808 set up a pewter shop in Meriden. Soon thereafter, he expanded his business by financing the employment of various local peddlers. Through the efforts of these peddlers, Griswold and other independent makers, a pivotal moment arrived in 1846 with the idea of a conglomeration of area silver manufacturers. However, it would take an additional six years to see action.

Two former Griswold peddlers, Horace C. and Dennis Wilcox, began to focus their creative efforts on the production of Britannia-metal. This alloy, with its silvery sheen and a resemblance to sterling silver, offered a more affordable alternative to the real thing. Although it had been in use since the mid-eighteenth century, with the scarcity of tin required in its composition, Britannia-ware was practically wiped from the market. Pewter briefly replaced it for a time but could not hold on in competition after tin became more plentiful. Britannia was more brilliant in appearance, harder and more resistant to wear. Additionally, it could take a high polish. For these reasons, peddlers found that their customers preferred it, and the demand for it grew rapidly after 1840.

A number of small shops were called on to meet this demand. Ashbil Griswold was producing Britannia-ware in North Meriden as early as 1830. James A. Frary and Couch & Benham made similar wares at a nearby Meriden plant. In East Meriden, Isaac C. Lewis, George Curtis and Darius Bingham Jr. made both pewter and Britannia products. The Curtises, Edwin E. and Lemuel J., were making Britannia-ware in their family shop on Curtis Street. Several other smaller Britannia and metal-ware shops were accounted for in Meriden, specifically in today's Britannia Street area, hence the name, but the biggest producer of Britannia-ware at the time was Charles Parker, Meriden's pioneer large-scale manufacturer.

The period was ripe for a combination of the Britannia enterprises, and the Wilcox brothers began to set the stage for further advancements in the industry. In December 1852, Horace C. and Dennis Wilcox of H.C. Wilcox & Company, Isaac C. Lewis of I.C. Lewis & Company, James A. Frary of James A. Frary & Company, Lemuel J. Curtis, William W. Lyman of Curtis & Lyman and John Munson of Wallingford organized the Meriden Britannia Company. Each of these businessmen was either mentored or had worked closely with the aforementioned Griswold. Months later, Samuel Simpson of Wallingford entered the group as an associate.

Horace and Dennis were especially interested in promoting sales, and their talents proved most effective. The first office and warerooms were in a building that stood at the corner of West Main and South Colony Streets; however, with its incredible early success, the company was able to fund its first building for finishing, assembling and plating on the southeast corner of State and Miller Streets. This plant was in operation by 1855, but until the 1860s, most of the actual manufacturing of the Britannia holloware was conducted in the many small individual plants taken over in 1852.

With the selling ability of Horace and Dennis Wilcox proving fruitful for the company and the elder Frary making frequent sales trips and arranging for the establishment of the various branches in large cities, the company flourished amazingly. In its first full year of operations, Meriden Britannia sold wares made by its own plants and purchased from other manufacturers amounting to more than $250,000 gross.

This circa 1860 photograph, captioned as the "Founders of Meriden Britannia Company," represents the dominating group behind the highly successful silver enterprise. *From the* Record-Journal.

Organized for quantity production, Meriden Britannia's first products were Britannia holloware, and by 1855, they were offering plated silver holloware and flatware and German silver articles. Pearl-handled wares were added in 1861.

By 1860, the company employed 320 hands and produced $500,000 worth of plated wares annually. Agencies had opened in New York, Chicago and San Francisco, and products were also shipped overseas. During this time, the metals of the business changed as well. Nickel-silver was now often being substituted for Britannia, and by the end of the decade, the company also offered sterling silver.

During this time, the Wilcox brothers became acquainted with another set of successful metalsmithing siblings—the Rogers brothers of Hartford. In 1847, the three brothers—Asa, Simeon and William Rogers—building on knowledge of methods already used in England, successfully developed and patented a new process in the plating of silver called electroplating. They imported German spoons and forks, which they were then able to coat with pure silver. The local peddlers were happy to add a supply of these table wares to their stock.

But by 1862, the Rogers brothers of Hartford were in financial difficulties. The Meriden Britannia Company soon bought their equipment, including the innovative tools and dies, and moved all of this material to Meriden from Hartford. This acquisition soon saw Meriden Britannia begin coating its products in silver through the electroplating process. Meriden products provided durability at an affordable price, which made the company a leading manufacturer of this type of metalware.

Upon the purchase, an arrangement was made with the Rogers brothers whereby they were to direct and supervise the manufacture of the company's 1847 Rogers Bros. silverplate line in the Meriden shop. Their 1847 Rogers Bros. trademark was an important addition to the Meriden Britannia Company, which now fully positioned itself as one of the largest and most prestigious silver companies in the world.

When the Civil War began, the conflict did not hamper the progress of the organization. It had just passed its first decade. What did affect progress, however, was that it needed more manufacturing space and equipment. On July 1, 1863, ground was broken on the west side of State Street for the company's first brick building. Soon, other large additions were made, including a building to house the power plant.

People were beginning to call the State Street plant the "Big Shop." Situated near the railway, in plain view of the traveler from New Haven to Hartford, Meriden Britannia covered a floor space of over ten acres and furnished employment within its brick walls to over 1,200. The main building was five hundred feet in length and an average width of sixty feet. It was five stories high, as were most of the buildings surrounding it. Elegantly appointed counting rooms, show rooms and packing looms were attached to the main building, while other large structures across the street were accessed by covered bridges and passages.

But there was still more than a trace of the primitive in the character of its trade. Many miscellaneous items were carried in their line, including tinware from Japan. Britannia shipments were made in exchange for fur, leathers or cordwood.

After the Civil War, Meriden experienced another period of rapid industrialization and urbanization. The growing railroad networks helped open up previously inaccessible markets in all parts of the region. The growth of industry in Meriden attracted thousands of workers from all over the world.

On July 16, 1870, a devastating fire destroyed the main building of the Meriden Britannia Company. The seven-hundred-foot-long building employed over nine hundred workers, including about one hundred women, all of whom were left temporarily without work. However, the building was fully insured, the loss was fully recovered and rebuilding began immediately. Work at the other six annexes was unaffected by the headquarters' fire. Up to this time, this fire was the worst to occur in Meriden history, although within months, the building was back in operation.

Since the acquisition of the Rogers Bros. trademark years prior, sales had risen rapidly, reaching a volume of $2.5 million annually by 1878. To care for the growing volume of business, a factory was erected in Hamiton, Ontario, Canada, in 1879 and placed under the management of J.H. Parker, formerly associated with various Meriden industries.

Meanwhile, the company's wares were winning favorable attention wherever they were displayed. In 1876, the Meriden Britannia Company made a significant impression at the Centennial Exposition in Philadelphia, winning the first-place medal for plated wares. Exhibitions continued for the company: New Orleans in 1885, Paris at the Universal Exposition in 1889 and the Columbian Exposition in Chicago in 1893, where it received high awards. By the last quarter of the century, Meriden Britannia Company was considered the largest silverware company in the world.

Early on, it was decided that co-founder Dennis Wilcox should devote most of his time to the business's New York interests. Although Dennis had built a costly mansion in Meriden, he sold it to his brother, Horace, about 1870. He opted to concentrate on balancing his time between the Empire State and Meriden. This, however, was short-lived; in 1879, Dennis Wilcox resigned as the treasurer of the company to become a speculator on Wall Street, thus moving to New York permanently. Due to the immense pressure of the occupation, Dennis Wilcox took his own life by way of a pistol in 1886 at the age of fifty-seven.

By the late nineteenth century, Meriden had become a hub for silver production. Numerous companies emerged in the area, specializing in various aspects of silver-plating and manufacturing. In 1898, a major consolidation took place with the formation of the International Silver Company. This manufacturing empire would prove to be the largest producer of silver goods in the United States, thus making Meriden remembered as the "Silver City." This behemoth company, headquartered in Meriden, had absorbed several smaller firms, including the Meriden Britannia Company.

The International Silver Company was formed on November 19, 1898. Thirteen independent companies, not including those in Canada, were consolidated to form the company. The next year, four were added and several more joined in the years that followed. The names of the companies participating in the consolidation into the International were the Meriden Britannia Company, including Hall, Elton & Company; Rogers, Smith & Company; Forbes Silver Company; Wilcox & Evertsen; Roges & Bros.; Middletown Plate Company; Wm. Rogers Manufacturing Company; Wilcox Silver Plate Company; Parker & Casper Company; Simpson, Hall, Miller & Company; Simpson Nickel Company; Meriden Silver Plate Company; Rogers Cutlery Company; Derby Silver Company; Manhattan Silver Plate Company; Holmes and Edwards Silver Plate Company; Barbour Silver Plate Company; Hartford Silver Plate Company; Roger & Hamilton Company; Norwich Cutlery Company; Watrous Manufacturing; E.G. Webster & Son; American Silver Company; Rowley Manufacturing Company; Southington Cutlery Company, silverware department; and Silver City Plate Company

International Silver dominated the American silver market for decades. Its innovative techniques, such as the reintroduction of 1847 Rogers Bros. brand, offered a wider variety of silver-plated goods to cater to different social classes. For decades, the Meriden factories hummed with activity, employing thousands of skilled workers in various stages of production.

During World War II, International Silver Company won the coveted Army-Navy "E" Award. However, in the 1950s and in response to overseas competition, International was made to diversify its metal work. This expansion continued into the 1960s when the company, now known as the abbreviated INSILCO Corporation, branched out into electronics, automotive components, office products and other facets.

The mid-twentieth century, however, saw a decline in the popularity of silver. Due to lower-priced imported silver, rising metal costs and the shifting of consumer preferences, a shrinking silver market soon followed. International Silver struggled to adapt, and by the late twentieth century, most of Meriden's silver factories had closed their doors. By 1984, silver production in Meriden had ended.

While the days of large-scale silver production in Meriden are over, the city's legacy lives on. Several historic buildings associated with the industry, like the International Silver Company Factory, stand as testaments to a bygone era. The skills honed during the silver boom continue to influence the city's manufacturing sector, albeit in different areas. Meriden,

Connecticut, has earned the nickname "The Silver City Capital of the World" for a reason.

Again, it's hard to believe that Meriden's great silverware industry had its origin on a peddler's cart.

12

Hanover's Hallowed Ground

A Short but Significant History of Camp Tyler and Its Regiments

The war spirit was in the air.

When the Southern guns opened fire on Fort Sumter on April 12, 1861, Connecticut's response was prompt and vigorous. As a staunch abolitionist state, it pledged its support to the Union. Meriden, too, answered the call immediately, looking for volunteers and slowly readying its public buildings with flags and bunting. Meetings were called to order on how the locals could pledge themselves to the effort. Money was quickly collected to outfit local troops as volunteers stepped forward to join the state's first regiments. In less than fifteen days, Meriden had a complete company of 77 men. Area towns heeded the call for soldiers too, and Connecticut's Governor William A. Buckingham proudly turned over two complete 780-man Connecticut regiments rather than one as requested from U.S. President Lincoln.

It was after the Union disaster at Bull Run, however, that Mayor William H. Mallory of Bridgeport obtained from Governor William A. Buckingham authority to recruit a squadron of Connecticut cavalry. At this early period of the war, the cavalry branch of the Union army was lamentably weak, and a plan was carried out to raise a regiment of twelve companies for the regular service.

On the Meriden homefront, an intense war meeting was held; industrialist Charles Parker presided, and Orville H. Platt, Dexter R. Wright, Reverend D. Henry Miller and G.H. Wilson made speeches in support of the local effort. It was determined that Meriden was to become host to a central Connecticut military encampment.

Land along the Quinnipiac River was secured, and construction began swiftly. Camp Tyler, Meriden's new training ground, was situated in West Meriden along the outskirts of the small village of Hanover, extending as far north as to today's Coe Avenue. It would play a significant role during the American Civil War, as the site served as preparatory grounds for soldiers, a hub for military activities and a reflection of the war's impact on the local community.

Of the twelve companies for regular service, the First Regiment Connecticut Volunteer Cavalry was originally a battalion of four companies—with one company coming from each congressional district in the state. The call for volunteers was issued on October 1, 1861, and once the companies were raised, a Colt revolver was presented to each man by Parker himself, in addition to their army-supplied weapon. A generous sum of $5,000 was also raised for the necessary equipment.

Within three weeks, the camp had been established. By October 22, 1861, Camp Tyler's open meadow had been transformed into a tented village. The volunteer cavalry, altogether 346 members strong hailing

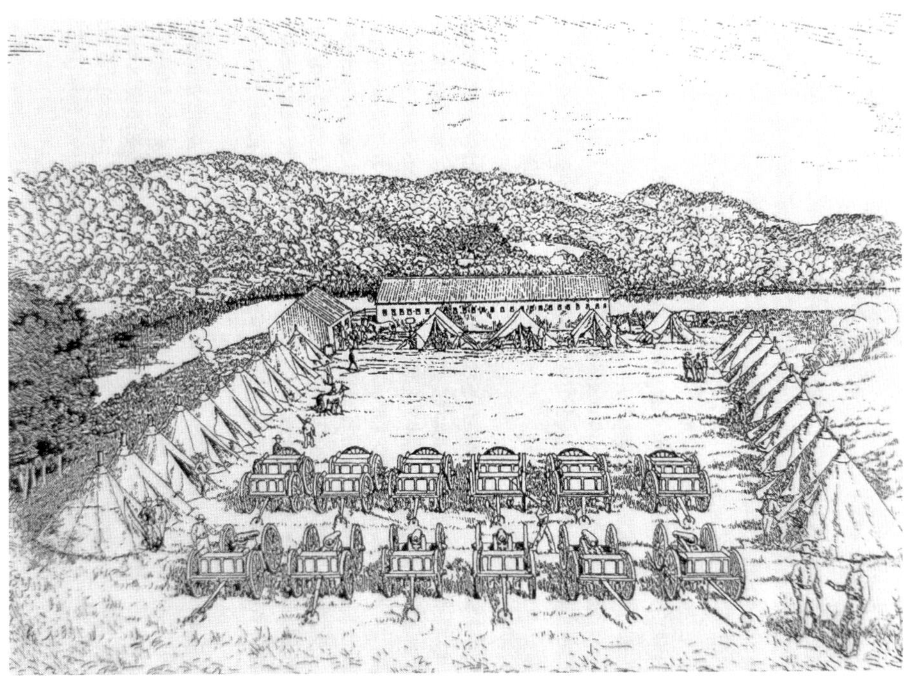

Camp Tyler (*illustrated here*) was home to Connecticut's First Light Battery's Civil War encampment in present-day South Meriden. *Meriden Historical Society.*

from Meriden, Wallingford, Southington or Cheshire, reported for roll, as the campfires warmed up coffee and soup. Stables for the horses were also quickly erected. Three days later, on a rainy evening, the horses arrived by car—restless, hungry and thirsty. Once settled, the battalion was out for a drill twice daily, often going through the town. An interested Connecticut Governor Buckingham and his wife visited the Meriden camp often.

Camp Tyler emerged as part of the Union's effort to prepare troops for battle. Named after Colonel Daniel P. Tyler, a prominent figure in the Connecticut militia, the camp provided essential training for soldiers from the state. Its location in West Meriden's Hanover section of town allowed easy access for recruits from surrounding vicinities to join its ranks.

Each morning, a bugle was heard throughout the village of Hanover. Camp Tyler bustled with activity as soldiers drilled tirelessly, learning the intricacies of musket warfare, marching formations and battlefield tactics. However, camp life was harsh, with soldiers enduring physical exertion, rudimentary living conditions and the ever-present threat of disease. Despite these hardships, a strong sense of camaraderie developed among the recruits as they prepared for the challenges ahead, and as the war intensified, the need for well-trained troops became paramount.

For recreation, the soldiers of Camp Tyler, as with all of the military men from both sides, were left to their own devices. Letter-writing, reading, singing, card-playing and sleeping were the favorite pastimes of the troops in camp. In the winter, men often constructed huts of logs and mud or piled dirt against the sides of their tents as insulation from the cold.

Beyond combat training, Camp Tyler hosted various support roles. Washerwomen, cooks and blacksmiths worked tirelessly to maintain the camp's functionality. These unsung heroes ensured that soldiers had clean uniforms, hot meals and well-maintained equipment.

The presence of Camp Tyler had a profound effect on Meriden's economy. Local businesses flourished as they supplied goods and services to the camp. Merchants, farmers and craftsmen benefited from the increased demand. One particular day, as the troops would often buy provisions and supplies from the local farmers and merchants, one thirsty party bought a barrel of cider at the Ivers family homestead on present-day Diamond Hill. The soldiers found that it was too heavy to carry. Instead, they decided that the easiest way to get it back to the camp was simply to roll the barrel down the length of the large hill. To the confusion and laughter of those witnessing this runaway barrel, it quickly broke away, and within moments, it rolled into the vicinity of the troops' barracks in the encampment.

Soldiers stationed at Camp Tyler interacted with Meriden's residents often. The exchange of stories, traditions and experiences bridged the gap between military life and civilian society. The camp became a melting pot of diverse backgrounds, fostering camaraderie and understanding.

While Camp Tyler brought economic benefits, it also exacted an emotional toll. As families bid tearful farewells to their loved ones as they left for war, the soldiers' days in the camp echoed with laughter, camaraderie and occasional sorrow. The letters exchanged between soldiers and their families revealed the heartache and longing that permeated daily life.

The artillery left the camp at the end of January 1862, and the cavalry of Camp Tyler, 346 men, departed West Meriden the following month, on February 20, 1862, for Wheeling, Virginia. Three days after arrival, on March 27, it was assigned to the brigade of General Robert C. Schenck and ordered to Moorefield, Virginia, to fight guerrillas.

As for the men of the Meriden troop, after they had left, the soldiers were put under Major Judson M. Lyon of Woodstock and took an active part in the Battle of McDowell on May 8, 1862, and in the Battle of Franklin on May 11 and May 12. Lyon had resigned in April 1862.

The company also served in the army of General Fremont, then in command of the Mountain Department, in his forced march across the mountains into the Shenandoah Valley to the relief of General Banks, participating in the Battles of Harrisonburg on June 6, Cross Keys on June 8 and Port Republic on June 9.

It subsequently took part in the arduous operations of the Army of Virginia under General Polk, participating in the various battles along the Rapidan and the Rappahannock and at Bull Run and Chantilly.

After nearly a year of constant activity, the battalion was assigned to duty at provost guard in the city of Baltimore, Maryland, and was increased to a full regiment of twelve companies. In February 1863, the regiment was attached to the Army of the Potomac and took an active part in all of its movements until August 8, 1864.

The regiment continued in service under Colonels Ives and Whittaker until August 2, 1865, performing gallant service, winning a well-merited reputation and doing honor to the State of Connecticut. The regiment fought many battles, with success in holding ground against General Stonewall Jackson at Wardensville, West Virginia, and at the Second Battle of Bull Run. The men were mustered out at Washington, D.C., on August 2, 1865, and left for New Haven for final discharge. The members of the regiment were permitted to take their horses with them to the state, a favor not granted to any other cavalry regiment.

Although Camp Tyler's lifespan was relatively short, it was not soon forgotten by the townsfolk. Once the cavalry left, the established Meriden Cutlery Company developed a dam and rearranged the waterway, which washed over the great meadows of the open fields, creating the soon-to-be seventy-acre Hanover Lake.

History alone cannot do full justice to the brave men who composed this magnificent regiment. Suffice it to say that it maintained a reputation for fidelity and bravery second to no other cavalry regiment in the war. Over the campaign, it engaged with the Confederate army more than eighty-five times, and four of its members received the Congressional Medal of Honor. The regiment escorted General Grant as he went to receive General Robert E. Lee's surrender at Appomattox, and it was later assigned to hunt for President Abraham Lincoln's assassin, John Wilkes Booth.

The average Civil War soldier, like those from Meriden, was a farm boy between eighteen and thirty who possessed little formal education by modern-day standards and whose military training was superficial.

No traces of the camp remain today, and only a small number of Civil War encampment markers have turned up. A marker bearing the inscription "Co. B 1864," indicating a tenting area for that company, resurfaced, as did markers that likely designated company streets.

Camp Tyler's legacy endures through historical records, artifacts and the stories retold from that tumultuous period. The Meriden encampment serves today as a reminder of sacrifice, resilience and the indomitable spirit of a nation at war. Also, it continues to stand as a testament to the courage and dedication of all Connecticut's soldiers during the Civil War.

Today, in addition to historical markers and local reenactments keeping the memory of the camp alive, a Civil War monument in front of Meriden's city hall lists all 158 men from the city who died during the War of the Rebellion. Overall, during the Civil War, 53,721 men served in Connecticut regiments, and there were about 20,000 casualties, including 4,891 deaths and 400 men missing.

It should be noted that the soldiers of the war had their horizons broadened by their travels to distant places. They emerged from their ordeal with a different understanding, as the word *union*, particularly, now meant nation, rather than state, or even North. It had taken four years of bitter campaigning to effect the transition. As expected, it would take time for the soldiers from Meriden and the surrounding areas to acclimate themselves as civilians once again. Rather than soldiers, they were now veterans.

While the physical remnants of Camp Tyler are largely absent from Meriden's landscape today, its legacy endures. Although the original site of the camp continues to be subject to many interpretations, Camp Tyler is believed to have existed along the southwestern edge of today's Hanover Pond, along the banks of Cutlery Street and today's Habershon Park.

13

Dr. Grove Herrick Wilson

The Father of the Free School System

All public schools of the town shall be free, and the expense of said schools, heretofore defrayed from the avails of rate bills, shall be paid by the town.
—Honorable Dr. Grove Herrick Wilson

Along one of the oldest and most populated city throughways stood the most unlikely of structures—the quaint, residential home of one of Meriden's most respected political and civic leaders—inserted into the center of an industry-run bustling downtown.

A former Meriden mayor, the Honorable Dr. Grove Herrick Wilson, was one of the area's leading local practitioners of the late 1800s. Born in Stockbridge, Massachusetts, in 1824, Wilson attended the local common schools and later studied in Massachusetts and Delaware, originally projected for a teaching profession. It was during his schooling, however, that he changed disciplines and became interested in medicine. This soon led to beginning studies at the Berkshire Medical Institution, from which he graduated in 1849; and two years later, he adopted the practice of homeopathy.

In 1857, Dr. Wilson relocated in Meriden, then a town of only three thousand. It was there that he set up his medical practice; two-thirds of the town's residents called him their physician. During his active practice, he achieved considerable fame by his contributions to medical journals, in which he was widely published and discussed. In 1882, he published a monograph in which he established the theory of the epidemic nature of intermittent fevers in New England.

In addition to his various lectures and presentations on natural science, Dr. Wilson expounded the principles of the telephone and phonograph two years prior to the production of these instruments by Edison. Dr. Wilson also invented an audiophone, an instrument that restores hearing to the deaf and a precursor to the hearing aid.

Notwithstanding the constant demands on his time, Dr. Wilson devoted considerable energy to the improvement of the educational system of the town. In fact, he is remembered as "the father of the free school system" for his persistent advocacy of the abolition of the "rate bill," which culminated in 1863, and who further motioned to make the Meriden schools absolutely free of charge for every child in the town. This effort would be monumental in American educational system history. Between 1840 and 1870, with the prodding of reformers, public financing evolved from a laissez-faire approach, where almost no tax money went toward education, to the rate-bill system, under which parents paid according to the number of children they had enrolled in the public schools, to a flat-rate system more closely

This Colony Street residence belonged to Dr. Grove Herrick Wilson, one of Meriden's most respected political and civic leaders. *Author's collection.*

resembling the one we are familiar with today. Dr. Wilson vehemently opposed the rate-bill system.

This monumental motion, carried largely through the influence of Wilson, along with Reverend John Parker and Welcome E. Benham, declared that "all public schools of the town shall be free, and the expense of said schools, heretofore defrayed from the avails of rate bills, shall be paid by the town."

This experimental plan of free schooling was met with universal favor. The Meriden school system quickly saw that the attendance increased; the finances were more simply and economically managed; and according to the Meriden Report of 1864, "the experience of the year [1863–1864] shows that this is the only just and proper method of securing to all of the benefits of a good education."

Two years later, the findings of these benefits induced the state legislature to extend the same privileges to all schools in the state.

Every public interest found a warm support in the doctor; and though he did not seek political honors, Dr. Wilson was asked into the political realm. Although he had been a member of the State Board of Health for many years, he also engaged in local affairs as the medical examiner for the town of Meriden. In 1880 and 1882, he was elected to represent Meriden in the General Assembly.

As support continued in the winter of 1892, Dr. Wilson was selected to head the Republican ticket in the city election. Although the city was Democratic by majority, Dr. Grove Herrick Wilson won, making him the city's mayor the following year.

Nearing seventy, Dr. Wilson fell victim to an onslaught of cardiac issues, namely an enlargement of the heart. As his health declined, he tried to remain active as a physician, but after forty-five years of practicing medicine in Meriden, Dr. Grove Herrick Wilson died on January 10, 1902.

14

THE GREAT MERIDEN RESERVOIR DEBATE

A Tale of Two Waters

Although Meriden had been a town in its own right since 1806, it was not until 1867 that it attained the status of incorporated city. With this incorporation badge, the city also gained additional municipal responsibilities. Newly elected Mayor Charles Parker and his staff quickly sprang into action. City officials, along with the approval of the recently formed Meriden Water Company, first had to amend the initial charter of the city before they were authorized to build the city's first waterworks in 1868.

Earlier in the decade, as the town gravitated toward its incorporation, officials began pondering the questions of a citywide water supply. Initial thought revealed that if the West Mountain rivers and brooklets—the area around today's Hubbard Park—could be pooled, there may be the potential of it being realized as a reservoir. The town's next move was to seek the advice of two brothers who were no strangers to the area or this water supply. Nathan and Joel Fenn, two well-known businessmen, lived on the opposite corners of today's West Main Street and Chamberlain Highway. Both were familiar with the territory, having traversed it from boyhood in every direction. They concluded that the area of this potential reservoir was a material basin and a previous site to one of the town's early cranberry marshes. Located partly in Meriden and Berlin, a dam was created (and aided by the local wildlife) along these waters, and the brothers began to witness the beginnings of a large pond. With the abundant mountain springs flowing into it from every direction, the area seemed an obvious choice for Meriden's initial reservoir.

Once the water had sufficiently accumulated (now called Lake Merimere), it was visited by such prominent citizens as Horace C. Wilcox and other members of the city's common council. These dignitaries sought to obtain chartered power from the next legislature to begin advancing the water supply's development. However, local industrialist and soon-to-be-first Meriden Mayor Charles Parker had input. He adamantly suggested that Meriden instead use the waters of Black Pond on the east side rather than the waters of West Mountain. This request began an incredibly long and arduous process for the city. In fact, even after the city was incorporated, with Parker at the helm, the agitation of the water question continued. Council appointed a committee, the new Meriden Water Company, and the services of an eminent hydraulic and civil engineer from Middletown to investigate and report.

As a result, the committee found that the West Mountain supply was four times greater than Black Pond. It also concluded that it would cost $50,000 to bring water from the mountain, whereas the total expense of the Black Pond project would be $250,000. The committee also reported that if Black Pond was selected, the city should pay Charles Parker $30,000 damages; I.C. Lewis and others a similar sum; and several other claimants along the line of Harbor Brook heavy amounts for damages done to their water privileges.

Luther Riggs was an astute publisher of the *Meriden Literary Recorder*, one of Meriden's earliest weekly newspapers. *Author's collection.*

On July 24, 1868, after a formal amendment to the charter was passed to permit needed construction to West Mountain, the new city government quickly sprang into action, mostly to the chagrin of Parker. However, Meriden soon found itself embroiled in a heated and escalating debate that would shape its future and test its power. Luther C. Riggs, the editor of the *Meriden Literary Recorder*, was strongly in favor of the Merimere, as were many on the city's common council; chief among the Black Pond supporters was Mayor Parker.

Charles Parker, Meriden's first mayor and a prominent nineteenth-century industrialist, vehemently debated against the present site of the Meriden reservoir in 1868. *Author's collection.*

Riggs, a Civil War veteran, was considered one of the strongest minds in the city but also one of questionable opinions. He, Parker and Parker family members feuded openly about an array of issues in and around Meriden—one could not count the number of attachments and criminal libel suits that were brought against him due to his actions through his newspaper. Riggs clashed with Parker through previous portrayals in the press, either written as a saint or as a sinner; it was a unique power struggle between two of Meriden's most influential. On one hand, Riggs, being publisher of the local newspaper, had major weight among many of the city residents, but Parker, too, was a stronghold.

Riggs decried that Parker wanted Black Pond as the source only because he and his partners owned substantial property among the pond's perimeters. They would ultimately benefit by the sale of land to the city for a watershed. Riggs continued by noting the Merimere's water quality was far superior to that of Parker's choice.

The battle of whether to put Meriden's first reservoir on the east side or west side was finally put to the citizens in a referendum. According to the *Meriden Daily Republican* on Tuesday, April 14, 1868, a committee was appointed with reference to the supply of water to the city, and it voted:

> *To petition the legislature at its May session 1868, for such an amendment of the city charter, as shall authorize the city to supply its inhabitants with pure and wholesome water, to be taken from any of the streams, springs, ponds, in the town of Meriden, or of any of the adjoining towns, and to issue bonds of the city for that purpose, and for any other amendments that may be necessary and proper to carry out such object, and that the clerk be authorized to sign such petition on behalf of the court of common council.*

On the eve of the vote, Riggs wrote in the *Meriden Recorder*:

> *The only question to be decided is whether you will have pure water from mountain springs and stream in the West Lake as recommended by eminent engineers, by three out of four water commissioners, and as voted by the Common Council by a three-fourths majority, or will you have impure water from a vast mudhole in the East as an expense of two hundred thousand dollars as urged by Black Pond spectaculars…* [who are] *flooding the city with circulars and handbills and are making a personal canvass, urging our people to vote for NO water. The idea of the East spectaculars is that they can't enrich themselves at the expense of the city, they will put a stop to all public improvements.*

The fight was a long and bitter one. The *Recorder* took the part of the taxpayers, fighting against what it termed the "Black Pond ring." The council committee reported in favor of the west side, with most voting in the same direction.

The vote was announced, and the reservoir of today, Merimere, was approved. This change seemed to inspire the community to take every measure or step it could to improve the appearance of Meriden. In his paper on April 14, 1869, Riggs wrote:

> *Last Saturday the citizens of Meriden achieved a signal, a complete victory over the Black Pond corrruptionist, the East Side mill-owners and land speculators.*
>
> *It is a victory jubilation of all creation.*
>
> *Victory! It is the burthen of our song, the boast of our speech, and will be of generations yet unborn, yea, as long as citizens of Meriden continue to drink water.*
>
> *Victory for the victorious sovereigns of Meriden who rejoice in the defeat and total annihilation of the Black Pond corrruptionist.*

Riggs was relentless in his public abuse of Charles Parker and, in later writings, even Parker family members, which ultimately sparked retribution.

One morning, hurrying for a train to Hartford and carrying a large bundle of editorial proof sheets, Luther Riggs was confronted by the mayor's son, Wilbur F. Parker.

"Parker alighting from his carriage, stepped before us, blocking the way, and finally demanded, 'Who wrote that d—— lie about me in yesterday's paper?'" Parker was referring to an article that Riggs had written the previous Saturday about the younger Parker being involved in an altercation.

Riggs responded with calm: "I never answer such questions put in such a manner. If the account was not correct, *The Recorder* will make the proper corrections."

"His reply was, 'D——n you, I don't want you to make any corrections. I will correct it myself,'" and without warning, as Riggs was helpless in holding the bundle, Parker struck him with a powerful blow to his left eye, drawing blood and now creating a public stir.

Parker then drew out from beneath his coat a short whip, with which he continued to strike Riggs. In a scene, Riggs wrestled Parker and managed to take the whip from him. Still bleeding, Riggs threw the whip to the ground, gathered his bundle and ran to the train, climbing aboard just as it was pulling out.

"Let Black Pond rejoice. Let Parker Avenue fire big guns, ring the bells, and hire the band to serenade the brave spirit who, armed with hevy [*sic*] cudgel, violently assaults an unsuspecting editor....It is a deed of valor."

But much of the populace of Meriden later believed that Wilbur Parker's actions were justified. After much publicity, the incident saw action. Wilbur Parker had submitted himself to the police court, where His Honor Andrew J. Coe inflicted a fine of $20 and costs for assaulting Riggs. Riggs threatened to sue Parker for $10,000, but no records have been found to prove he proceeded with the claim. He did, however, use his literary connections to publicize the assault on him. News of the attack was published in newspapers of Hartford, New Haven, Bridgeport, Waterbury and other Connecticut cities.

Charles Parker countered with a suit against Riggs for libel, as did others who swore to have also been tormented, some ten in all. Finally, there was a compromise. Parker settled with those who had sued Riggs instead of any damages he might have to pay for assault. There was peace afterward.

With the West Mountain location approved, construction of Merimere, Meriden's first reservoir, began in June 1869. Within six months, on Christmas Day 1869, Meriden had completed a gravity system that would be operational using cement wrought-iron pipes supplying the city water from the West Mountain reservoir. The Merimere Reservoir was in its infancy. It wasn't fully operational until 1873, and even then, the local service water was mostly confined to the west side. In just four years' time, it was reported that 1,554 families were being served with water through pipes of the city's new system.

For years following the dispute, the reservoir debate continued to be discussed in civic circles and throughout the community. In fact, it is stated that for the remainder of his life, Charles Parker never gave up hope of the Black Pond waters becoming a city reservoir. Parker died on January 31, 1902, in Meriden at the age of ninety-three.

15

THE ENDURING LEGACY OF SERVICE

Exploring the Edwin J. Merriam Post 8 in Meriden

I am willing to give up all of my worldly interests and enjoyments, if I can thereby secure the invaluable blessings of universal justice and freedom to those who shall live after me.
—Lieutenant Edwin J. Merriam, as told to Captain Eaton of the Union army

Woven into the historical tapestry of Meriden lies the Edwin J. Merriam Post No. 8, a chapter of the Grand Army of the Republic. The Merriam Post No. 8's story transcends the local level. It is a microcosm of the broader national narrative of veteran support and the evolution of veterans' organizations; the story of the Merriam Post No. 8 extends well beyond the Civil War era.

The Grand Army of the Republic (GAR) was established in 1866 and served as a fraternal organization for Union army veterans of the Civil War. Local chapters, known as posts, provided space for veterans to reconnect, share their experiences and advocate for veterans' rights. The Meriden GAR post, one of the oldest and most influential in the state department, was chartered in 1876 and named after a local Civil War hero, Colonel Edwin J. Merriam.

The first meeting at which steps were taken for organizing the post was held at the residence of Reverend J.J. Woolley, pastor of Center Congregational Church, in January 1867. Reverend Woolley had been chaplain in the Eighth Connecticut Company during the Civil War and was in thorough sympathy with the Grand Army movement. This well-attended meeting was the impetus of a Meriden post.

This Merriam Post No. 8, GAR letterhead features its namesake, Lieutenant Edwin J. Merriam of the Seventh Connecticut Regiment. *Sherwin Borsuk.*

The Merriam Post was organized in February 1867 in the armory of the Meriden Veteran Guards in the town hall building. The veterans quickly took interest in the GAR affairs and selected delegates to attend the first state convention in Hartford on April 11 of that year. Once organized, the post received its charter four days later on April 15, 1867, and was divided into four districts, with Colonel Charles L. Upham of Meriden appointed to command the second district.

The first convention of the GAR posts in the state was held in Meriden on August 11, 1867, for the purpose of organizing the Connecticut Department. Delegates were present from the Meriden post. However, with Meriden now granted a post, the chapter's next order of business was to bestow a name on it. This was customarily reserved to honor a fallen soldier from the town.

The following year, on November 16, 1868, a vote was cast to decide a name for the post. The vote resulted in a unanimous adoption of "Merriam" in honor of Second Lieutenant Edwin J. Merriam.

Edwin J. Merriam was born on March 25, 1833, in Meriden, removing to Durham, Connecticut, before enlisting on August 28, 1861, as a sergeant. He was mustered into Company C of the Seventh Connecticut Infantry on September 6, 1861, and afterward reenlisted, being promoted on December 22, 1863, to commissary sergeant. Quick to move up in the ranks, he was promoted once again to second lieutenant of Company E on April 12, 1864. While leading his company at the Battle of Deep Run, Virginia, on August 16, 1864, where their strategy was to secure their hold on the Wilmington & Weldon Railroad, Lieutenant Merriam was severely wounded below the knee.

Rallying his men and bidding them to stand together and fight for the old flag, Merriam was left behind. He was too weak to allow the amputation of his limb, and his sufferings were extreme. His surgeon and all who met him in the hospital regarded Merriam as a marvel of patience and endurance.

Lieutenant Merriam died at Chesapeake Hospital, near Fortress Monroe, on October 5, 1864. His remains were brought to Meriden, and a funeral was held in the First Congregational Church, of which he was a member. Both Reverend H.C. Hayden and Reverend Jacob Eaton, chaplain of the Seventh Connecticut Volunteers, took part in the services. The Union Guard performed a military escort to the grave in West Cemetery, and the deceased soldier was buried with honors.

On February 29, 1868, an order from the National GAR Headquarters abolished the districts in the state department and ordered that all posts in the state take their rank and number from the dates on their charters. This resulted in Merriam Post receiving No. 8 in the line of seniority.

Members of the Merriam Post No. 8, GAR, proudly stand outside their headquarters in Meriden on August 11, 1890. *Meriden Historical Society.*

Coincidentally, since Meriden accounted for such a large GAR membership, an additional post, No. 15, was also added to the city.

During its heyday, Merriam Post No. 8 hosted many social functions, political speeches, fundraisers and other community activities. Many of these events took place at the GAR Hall located at 9–11 Colony Street. Membership peaked at 302 members and included representatives from the army and navy.

Throughout the late nineteenth and early twentieth centuries, the Merriam Post No. 8 played a vital role in Meriden's social fabric. The post organized annual Memorial Day observances, honoring fallen soldiers and reminding the community of the sacrifices made during the Civil War. These solemn events fostered a sense of patriotism and civic duty among residents. Beyond commemorative events, the post actively supported veterans and their families. It lobbied for government pensions for veterans and widows, ensuring financial security for those who had served their country. The post also provided a social network for veterans, offering camaraderie and support during a time when the wounds of war were still fresh.

As the Grand Army of the Republic began to decline in membership and Civil War veterans passed away, the spirit of the post lived on. In many communities, the posts evolved into broader veterans' organizations, encompassing veterans of subsequent wars. The Merriam Post was disbanded in 1940 after its last surviving member, Charles S. Gallager, died at the age of ninety-six. The GAR Hall was then purchased in 1941 by Samuel L. Beloff and made into a retail outlet.

The legacy of the Edwin J. Merriam Post No. 8 is multifaceted. It serves as a historical marker, reminding us of the sacrifices made by Civil War veterans, and provides a lasting tribute to honor those who have served our nation. Colonel Merriam's story embodies the spirit of sacrifice and service that the post aimed to uphold.

The history of the Merriam Post No. 8 offers a deeper understanding of the experiences of Civil War veterans after the war. The stories and experiences of the Civil War veterans' reintegration after the war and into society, their advocacy for veterans' rights and their creation of support networks offer valuable insights into the social and political landscape of the late nineteenth century.

16

A Capital Ambition

Meriden's Bid for Connecticut's Heart in the 1860s

Connecticut, one of the smallest states in the union,
plainly needs but one State House.
—Meriden Transcript, *June 7, 1855*

The state capitol in Hartford, capped by its golden dome and adjacent to the beautiful forty-one-acre Bushnell Park, became the official seat of Connecticut's state government in 1879. But for Meriden, this site would come after much consideration and hope, suspense and finally disappointment. Although Meriden has had a rich history that extends beyond its well-known label as the Silver City and its manufacturing prowess, it once harbored the unique aspiration of becoming the state capital.

The Connecticut Colony and the New Haven Colony were two separate colonies until 1662, when a charter from King Charles II united them. Hartford was the only capital of the new unit until 1701; however, from 1701 to 1874, there were two capitals in Connecticut: New Haven and Hartford. Originally, both cities assumed respective responsibilities within the Connecticut government, but the General Assembly always met in Hartford. Over time, biannual General Court meetings began to take place: each May in Hartford and each October in New Haven. Even after Connecticut achieved statehood in 1788 and it adopted its constitution in 1818, meetings of the General Court continued to alternate between the two cities.

As early as the mid-nineteenth century, Connecticut state officials began to witness a disconnect between their two state delegations. Ultimately, this disconnect would be the catalyst for a proposal of combining the two statehouses. For the record, a study into a suitable sole-capital space in Connecticut began as early as 1855, but it was in 1866 that the General Assembly appointed commissioners to fully investigate the matter more closely. Each city clearly had its advantages. New Haven had a larger population, more industry and more wealth, but Hartford had a more centralized location and was a financial and insurance center.

The 1860s were a period of immense change for the United States. The Civil War had reshaped the nation, and Connecticut, a burgeoning industrial center, was no exception. Amid this transformation, a bold proposition emerged: Could the state capital remove to Meriden? In fact, in addition to Meriden being considered, neighboring Middletown was considered, but to a lesser degree. Both of these options served as a viable solution to a long-standing idea to have a more-centralized location for its state capital as opposed to the two co-capitals, New Haven and Hartford.

But this debate over the capital transcended mere location. It reflected the evolving political and social landscape of Connecticut. The rise of industrial towns like Meriden challenged the traditional dominance of established, often more rural, areas. Meriden's bid could be seen as an attempt by the state's growing industrial sector to assert its influence. Conversely, Hartford's resistance reflected a desire to preserve the existing power structure. But, more importantly, Meriden's central position offered better accessibility to both capital cities, allowing legislators to convene without favoring one region over the other. Moreover, its proximity to major transportation routes—railroads and highways—further enhanced its appeal.

Meriden's central position wasn't just about geography. It symbolized a new era for Connecticut. Hartford, situated on the state's periphery, was seen by some as reflecting a bygone agricultural past. Meriden, on the other hand, embodied the dynamism of the Industrial Revolution. Proponents argued that a centrally located capital would be more accessible to a wider range of citizens, fostering a more representative government.

Despite Meriden's compelling arguments, Hartford's supporters countered with their own. Hartford had served as the capital since Connecticut's colonial days. It possessed established infrastructure, including a state capitol building and a network of government offices. Uprooting this deeply embedded system, argued Hartford's defenders, would be disruptive and expensive. Additionally, Hartford's historical significance held symbolic weight. It was seen as a repository of the state's legacy, a quality Meriden—a young city—couldn't replicate.

Throughout a succession of state- and city-led meetings, it was decided that a site and a plan was needed in order for Meriden's consideration to continue. The proposed site of the Connecticut State Capitol in Meriden was intended to be on land bounded by present-day Columbus, Highland, Meriden and Prospect Avenues. Atop this overlook, boundaries on Columbus Avenue and Highland Avenue had no residences; however, the other tracts had adjacent properties that would need to be cleared if used.

As the idea of the town becoming Connecticut's newest capital surfaced and the buzz on the Meriden streets increased, the prospect of hosting the state government ignited hopes and dreams. The city's leaders envisioned grand government buildings, bustling legislative sessions and newfound prominence. Plans were carefully drawn up, readying for the potential approval to come to fruition.

It was a transitional period for the city. In addition to the pending capital decision, Meriden was officially incorporated as a city in 1867. With this newest accreditation, Meriden residents grew optimistic with each passing day as the proposal to become the state capital gained momentum. On the streets, citizens debated the merits, often envisioning a transformed Meriden—a place where laws would be crafted, debates held and history made.

In 1869, Connecticut positioned its legislative committee to once again consider the effectiveness and future of the multi-capital system. Unfortunately, the choice of Meriden ultimately failed. It was determined that it faced infrastructure limitations. Its roads, public buildings and utilities were not adequately prepared to accommodate the demands if it were granted Connecticut's state capital. And while compelling arguments were made, the inertia of tradition and the logistical challenges of relocation proved too strong.

In the end, it was the City of Hartford that offered up a plot of land and a $500,000 check to construct its new capitol, an offer residents could not turn down. The public took it to a vote, and in 1875, Hartford was named the sole capital city of Connecticut.

Meriden's attempt, however, was not unfelt. The city had left its mark. It highlighted the state's changing demographics and the growing importance of its industrial centers. The debate served as a reminder of the dynamism inherent in American politics, where established centers of power are constantly challenged by rising forces.

It can be written that Meriden's dream went unfulfilled. The state capital remained elsewhere, leaving Meriden to focus on its industrial prowess. Although Meriden missed out on the capital title, it continued to thrive. The city's factories churned out silverware, earning it the nickname the "Silver City." Today, Meriden's brief flirtation with state capital status remains a captivating tale. While it didn't wear the gubernatorial crown, it etched its name in history as a dynamic, industrious community—one that embraced change and forged its own path.

CITY OF...

17

The Enigma of the Leatherman

Unveiling the Story of a Connecticut Wanderer

Occasionally, legend and reality unite in the form of some remarkable soul who, through peculiarity or chance, assumes a role resembling the mythical characters we read about in childhood's fairy tales. The Leather Man was one of these.
—Allison Albee, 1937

There is no traveling man more well known than the Leatherman.

The figure of the Leatherman, a solitary wanderer, clad in homemade leather garments, has haunted the historical landscape of Connecticut and New York for over a century. His story endures today as a local legend shrouded in mystery and speculation.

Although no one knew for sure his real name, what was assured was that this strange and silent figure trudged through rural Connecticut, Massachusetts and New York State from about 1856 until his death in 1889.

This wanderer was about 5'7" and weighed about 140 pounds. He had a high and commanding forehead, black hair and a short black beard and dark blue-gray eyes. His complexion was quite dark, either naturally or from exposure, but it was his clothing the world would remember. His rude clothing was made of soft tanned calfskin leather, stitched together with thongs. He wore a long coat with pockets both inside and out, fitted from the crown of his head to the soles of his thick, wood-soled, leather-topped boots. A cap with a leather visor completed his costume—made entirely of leather—which he manufactured himself from small scraps given to him by kindhearted people he visited.

The Leatherman was a mysterious figure who walked a circuit in the northeastern United States between the Connecticut and Hudson Rivers from roughly 1857 to 1889. *Meriden Historical Society.*

Under his left arm he carried a large leather knapsack containing many items, such as cigar stumps he would have picked up along the country roads of his journey, often only to be traded in at a tobacco store on his next stop for sewing thread. He also always carried an awl for working leather.

He was a French Canadian and fluent in French. Oftentimes, he communicated mostly with grunts and gestures, rarely using his broken English. It can be presumed that he was born around 1839, as determined by the coroner's inquest after his death. This finding would have put his age at about fifty years old at that time, and from this, it can be deduced that he would have been about seventeen to nineteen years old when he began his trek, which was first reported in Connecticut and New York about 1856 to 1858. There is further evidence—the intricacy of stitch patterns found on his leather overcoat and the arrangement of items found in a majority of his caves—to suggest the Leatherman may have suffered from obsessive-compulsive disorder.

He lived and traveled alone, sleeping in a rotating series of crude lean-tos and caves in and around the forests. These caves were quite an interesting aspect of the Leatherman story. Some of them have been excavated by archaeologists; today, many of them, in parks scattered throughout the area he roamed, are marked and still regularly visited.

The Leatherman routinely sheltered in the caves of his visited towns. Living in these rock shelters and "Leatherman caves," as they are now locally known, he was often labeled as a hobo or tramp, although he was never found to have stolen anything or have begged, molested or hurt anyone. He did, however, freely take anything given or offered to him. In 1879, both New York and Connecticut enacted "Tramp Laws," which allowed authorities to arrest any homeless person who wandered the area after the end of the Civil War. Although the Leatherman was not exempt from these regulations, he was arrested only once. Everyone knew him, and they knew he wasn't dangerous. In fact, one account remembers that the Leatherman had somewhat of a playful side. One time, a group of children left four tarnished pennies on a fence post; the Leatherman pocketed them and replaced them with four shiny new ones.

Although he refused to interact on a personal level, there are at least seventeen different photos of him, as he posed often for curious townspeople.

The mystery of the Leatherman's origins and identity swirled for decades, and it has never been fully revealed. In fact, one tentative identification was discovered to be a hoax.

In 1884, W.A. Sailson, a reporter for the *Waterbury Daily American*, published a devastating story under the headline "The Mystery Solved." This story was later found to be a hoax perpetrated by a journalist, William A. Gordon, a Woodbury, Connecticut resident. His family owned the former Gordon's Tannery, where the Leatherman visited for the oiling of his outfit. It would be here that Gordon witnessed the legendary traveler often. William's younger brother Alexander, however, became jealous of William's rise to popularity with his writing, especially in his coverage of the Leatherman, and Alexander made up a fictitious story about the old Leatherman.

The concocted backstory said that the Leatherman was born Jules Bourglay, likely in Lyons, France, and as a young man he had fallen in love with the daughter of a rich leather merchant. The father, who initially disapproved of the proposed match, agreed that Bourglay could marry his daughter if, after a year's trial in the family business, he proved his worth. Unfortunately, as tradition states, Bourglay was entrusted with a business dealing that went bad, and the family lost their fortune. Heartbroken and ashamed, he immigrated to America, where he embarked on circular routes, wandering aimlessly through the countryside and wearing his leather suit as a penance for his failures.

The story proved to be so realistic, full of romance and adventure, that it was used and reprinted in several other papers. Before long, it was being accepted as fact, even though the newspaper in which it had originally appeared confirmed that it was completely fictitious. In fact, Alexander Gordon later admitted within twenty-four hours of the Leatherman's death in 1889 that he had fabricated the wanderer's identity and past.

Around 1883, the Leatherman began to travel a precise route: a clockwise circuit of 365 miles through northern Westchester and Putnam Counties in New York and adjacent areas in Connecticut. He completed the loop every thirty-four days, appearing in certain villages with such punctuality that residents were said to set their clocks by the time of his arrival. He would travel this same route for the rest of his life.

Throughout his travels, the Leatherman was something of a nineteenth-century celebrity. When he was slated to arrive in a town, teachers would dismiss school and all of the children would go outside, stand by the fences and watch him go by.

Chauncey Hotchkiss, a regular townsperson of Forestville, Connecticut, made note of the peculiar man suited in leather. Hotchkiss was interested in and decided to trace the route of the Leatherman. He noticed that he seemed to arrive every thirty-four days. This was proven, and in July 1885, the *Hartford Globe* published a timetable of the Leatherman's schedule and used Hotchkiss's route calculations.

The Leatherman knew how to take care of himself. He carved troughs at the base of chestnut trees to help preserve beef. He grew his own gardens. Since his route revolved, he even planted seeds to be harvested in future trips. He dug holes to preserve apples, nuts and berries. His caves were all quite ingenious in layout, too. In them, he engineered a secondary outlet to promote oxygen flow and prevent asphyxiation. In the winter, he likely survived blizzards and other foul weather by heating his rock shelters with fire. While his face was reported to be frostbitten at times due to the cold, by the time of his death, he had not lost any fingers, an unfortunate trend other tramps of the time may have endured.

By 1886, sightings of the Leatherman referenced a growth on his lip that ultimately turned out to be cancerous. The towns began to openly speak of the growth and feared it needed medical attention. During the blizzard of 1888, when the Leatherman was held up in Southington, he disappeared for several days, and the locals feared that he was dead. In fact, townspeople started calling for his capture so he could be treated. The local Humane Society determined that he could no longer care for himself, and a warrant was issued for his arrest.

In December of that year, Humane Society agent Richard DeZeng caught up with the Leatherman in present-day Middletown, Connecticut, where the vagabond was willingly bundled into a carriage bound for Hartford Hospital. Although the staff was instructed to oversee him, the Leatherman escaped and resumed his travels alone.

In addition to the open sore now covering much of his face, he seemed to be moving unsteadily, and he failed to keep his strict schedule. In his final days, he went off of his normal route, likely looking for a physician. He went to a doctor's house in Reading; the doctor was out, but his wife was home and spoke fluent French. The Leatherman was clearly suffering from lip cancer and told her he could not eat solid foods. She reciprocated with a liquid meal. Unfortunately, while conversing comfortably, the wife asked about his backstory. He immediately got up, obviously offended, and left the home.

On March 24, 1889, the Leatherman's nomadic lifestyle came to an end. He was found in a cave about one thousand feet from the road on the George Dell Farm in Mount Pleasant, New York. At the inquest, the coroner identified him simply as "the Leatherman" and estimated his age to be about fifty years. It was also determined that he had died four days earlier, on March 20, from blood poisoning due to cancer. He was buried the following day.

Along with his remains, several other items were recovered from his leather satchel: a tobacco pipe, a frying pan, a knife, a small tin pail, an awl, a French prayer book, a crucifix and a paper code of sorts. Later, these items were removed to White & Dorsey's undertaking rooms in Ossining, New York, where many curious visitors viewed his body. Nearby was the rugged and worn sixty-pound leather suit that gave him his name. It was later determined that he carried almost half of his body weight in the leather garment he wore and the baggage that he bore.

Shortly after his death, Eden Musee Waxworks on West Twenty-Third Street in Manhattan, New York, obtained the Leatherman's suit from the funeral director with the hope they could use it on a wax figure of the Leatherman. Unfortunately, the Eden Musee went bankrupt and closed in 1915, and all of its assets were frozen. A short time later, the name and select wax figure groupings, including those from the Chamber of Horrors, were purchased at auction and exhibited in Coney Island. Alas, the Coney Island Eden Musee, including the Leatherman's suit, was destroyed by fire in 1928.

For sixty-four years after his death, a plumbing pipe stuck into the ground was the only marker for his grave in Ossining's Sparta Cemetery in New York. However, in 1953, a headstone was placed on the spot, identifying the deceased as the then believed Jules Bourglay. But on May 25, 2011, his grave's contents were exhumed and reburied at a new site in the cemetery; however, no visible human remains were recovered during the exhumation. Only coffin nails and soil from the original burial plot were reburied in the new grave. One of the reasons for the exhumation was the hope that any remains could help determine the Leatherman's origins. Today, a stone and brass marker on the grave simply states, "The Leatherman."

Today, the Leatherman's story exists at the intersection of fact and fiction. The lack of personal records and his deliberate secrecy make it difficult to separate historical truth from embellished folklore. However, the enduring power of his legend lies in its ability to spark imagination and connect us to the past.

18

FROM PATCH CORDS TO PROGRESS

The First Commercial Telephone Exchanges in the World

The telephone, a revolutionary invention that forever altered communication, wouldn't have reached its full potential without the humble switchboard. This seemingly simple device, a central hub connecting individual lines, laid the groundwork for our modern interconnected world.

The first commercial telephone exchange in the world began operations on January 28, 1878, in a storefront of the Boardman Building in New Haven, Connecticut. Civil War veteran and manager for the Atlantic and Pacific Telegraph Company George Willard Coy designed and built the world's first switchboard for commercial use. Influenced by Alexander Graham Bell's lecture and demonstration of his new invention, the telephone, at the Skiff Opera House in New Haven on April 27, 1877, Coy's success in achieving the first switchboard proved monumental.

During Coy's January 28 public demonstration of his switchboard, Ellis B. Baker Sr. of Meriden was among the many spectators in the audience. Baker was interested in making a switchboard, and on speaking with Coy, Baker immediately received permission to make a replica of Coy's innovation. In fact, Coy even furnished the drawings.

Baker was an ingenious and enterprising individual. He was born in Winsted, Connecticut, where he worked briefly as a printer and store clerk. In 1872, then all of eighteen years old, he moved to Meriden and became paymaster at the Edward Miller Company in Meriden. He also worked as the telegraph operator for the Atlantic and Pacific Telegraph Company, whose lines, coincidentally, served the Miller Company.

Working with William C. Homan, a young machinist at the Miller Company, Baker built two telephones, the first two phones in Meriden. One was in Homan's 174 Curtis Street home and the other of a Crown Street resident. This innovative feat was the world's first house-to-house phone line. These phones were connected by wooden poles with brass wires attached to porcelain knobs.

Baker also recruited the help of Roger D. Blish to help with what would later become the oldest and most famous existing telephone switchboard in the world. The primitive single-line connections between the two instruments worked well, but what was needed was a switchboard or some device to connect other phones. Baker mounted four circles of carriage bolts on a black walnut panel, forty inches wide and thirty inches high. In the center of each circle was a switch that could be moved from carriage bolt to carriage bolt, each connected by a wire in the rear to a subscriber's telephone line. Ironically, the switch lever handles were improvised from teapot cover knobs manufactured by the aforementioned Miller Company.

It was finished and operational within three days, and Baker formally opened his telephone exchange from a rear room of a business on Colony Street. The date, as he later recalled, was January 31, 1878, which would place it just three days after the New Haven opening. A description of the original article in the *Meriden Journal* for April 13, 1925, stated:

> *This first telephone exchange was located in the office of A.L. Stevens, real estate and insurance broker, whose place of business was about where Fred Weber's jewelry store now is. The telephone exchange was on the Railroad Avenue side of the building. When the Byxbee block was erected, the building was moved to Lewis Avenue, and converted into a dwelling house. Today, it stands as the first house south of the ballfields on the west side of the street.*

Another Meriden newspaper article followed:

> *There were a few local telephones in Meriden even before Mr. Baker set up his first switchboard though. The very first of these was a line from the house of E.B. Baker on Broad Street to W.M. Quested's house. This was later extended to Judge Fay's house, and then to W.R. Rigg's*

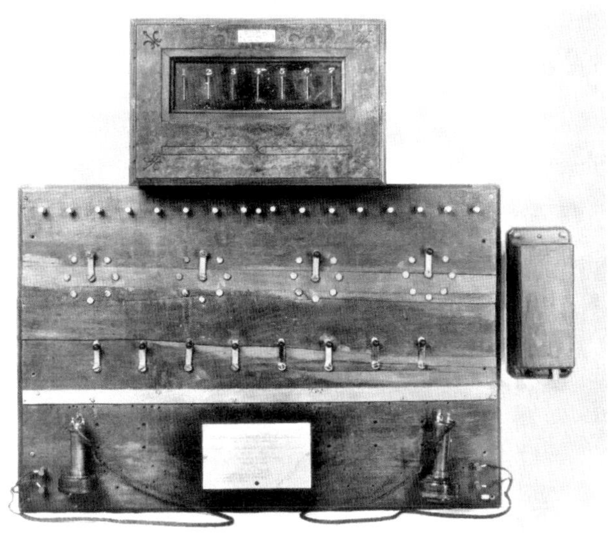

Meriden's first telephone exchange, opened in 1878, was the second commercial exchange in the world, only preceded by one in New Haven. *AT&T Archives and History Center.*

> *and George Coan's. The factory of the Edward Miller Company was the first one to be equipped, and the first long local-line was from the Charles Parker Company's office on Elm Street to the Parker Spoon Shop over east.*

Shortly after the opening of the Colony Street office, the exchange was moved to 10 Railroad Avenue, where Baker also carried on a small coal business. Even in those days, the question of telephone competition was in existence. In fact, George H. Santy, the manager of the Western Union Telegraph office in Meriden at that time, did his best to persuade prospective telephone subscribers that the telephone service would be far less useful than the district messenger box system. Interestingly, Santy later became manager of the very exchange that he originally did his utmost to defeat.

Progress was slow and steady, as the city was not large, and Meriden seemed to have taken kindly to the telephone. When Baker published the first directory on February 28, 1878, a month after the service was first offered, forty-seven subscribers were listed. This directory and the one issued at New Haven about the same time are the oldest telephone directories in the world.

As interest in the exchange progressed at an alarmingly healthy rate, Baker saw that the business could bring in top dollar. On December 3, 1878, under letterhead quaintly titled, "Ellis B. Baker, Dealer in Coal and Wood, and Manager of District Telephone Co. No. 1 Railroad Ave.," he wrote to Herrick Frost, a prominent New Haven businessman and backer to the New Haven District Telephone Company, offering to sell the exchange and all of the equipment for $800.

Instead, however, in the fall of the following year, the business of the Meriden District Telephone Company was sold to the Western Union Telegraph Company on Meriden's Winthrop Square. But another change of hands soon came, and in 1880, when Western Union patent claims were denied, the Meriden exchange was acquired by a New Haven group, the Connecticut Telephone Company. Baker later joined this company as general superintendent and saw the company redesign itself once more two years later, in 1882, as it became the Southern New England Telephone Company.

Before the conversion in 1881, Baker became superintendent of the Connecticut Telephone Company, in active charge of the development of service throughout the state. He devoted the greater part of his business life to the telephone, originated many new methods of construction and types of service and was, in the fullest sense of the word, a telephone *pioneer*.

Telephone numbers were not used then. Calls were made by giving the operator the name of the family or business place wanted. Operators then either memorized the lines at their switchboard or checked their own list of names if they were doubtful. Oftentimes, operators of the early days were boys and young men who delighted in playing pranks with the instruments and wholeheartedly enjoyed a rousing good argument with an irate subscriber. Indeed, invitations with face-to-face encounters to settle the arguments were not at all unusual. In the first years, telephones were used principally for business purposes. Only 39 families in the city of approximately 20,000 had telephones at home, and 7 of those were doctors. For the somewhat primitive telephone service they received, Meriden residents paid eighteen dollars a year and also bore the cost of running wires to their homes or offices. However, by 1882, four years after the exchange opened, the Connecticut Telephone Company listed 145 subscribers in the Meriden area. Of these, 132 were in Meriden, 9 in Wallingford, 2 in South Meriden and 1 each in Yalesville and East Meriden. Four "pay stations" were listed separately: one at the telephone office at Wilcox Block, one at the A.L. Stevens office, one at the uptown post office on East Main Street and one at the Metropolitan Wringer Office in Middlefield.

It was in 1888, when the number of Meriden phones had grown to about 235 and New Haven had more than 1,000, that the telephone company decided it was time to start listing numbers in the directory. It urged customers to call by number but did not make it obligatory until a year or two later. This disturbed a good many people, among them an editor of the local newspaper, the *Meriden Republican*, who felt it was his "duty to the public" to protest in favor of the operators, noting, "Every domestic in families cannot readily find numbers in a directory, while she can readily give the name of a party wanted." The conclusion could be drawn that phones were still considered a luxury, as they were found only in households affluent enough to have domestic help.

For years following, the city's telephone lines progressed in abundance: the 1,000 mark was passed in 1905, 3,000 in 1914 and 6,500 in 1926. As Meriden's telephone development continued an upward trend, regulations on rates and services needed to be appended for Southern New England Telephone and other utilities. By 1911, a Public Utilities Commission had been created, and with this help, the Meriden telephone company continued to grow rapidly throughout the first years of the twentieth century and beyond.

Ellis B. Baker Sr. lived in Meriden for many years as general superintendent of the Southern New England Telephone Company. He retired in 1913 and died five years later in 1918. His private office walls were decorated with pages from his first Meriden telephone directory. His son, also named Ellis B. Baker, followed and later became the vice president, secretary and treasurer of Southern New England Telephone, retiring in 1941 and passing two years later.

Although New Haven's original switchboard has been lost due to dismantlement, the original switchboard used in the first Meriden telephone exchange of 1878 was on loan in the Smithsonian Institution in Washington, D.C., for years. Afterward, the Meriden board was later displayed at a Bell System historical exhibit in New York City, but today, it proudly is housed in the AT&T Archives and History Center in Warren, New Jersey.

The influence of the first telephone switchboards transcended mere communication. They fostered the growth of businesses, facilitated emergency response and brought a sense of connection to geographically dispersed communities. The switchboard operator became a familiar and often friendly voice, a human touch in an increasingly technological world. It remains as a testament to human ingenuity and its ability to adapt to changing needs. From the basic manual systems to the revolutionary automatic exchanges, the switchboard laid the groundwork for our modern telecommunication infrastructure. While the iconic image of the switchboard operator has faded with the rise of digital technology, its legacy lives on in the interconnected world we take for granted today.

Not unlike the history of the city, the story of the telephone in Meriden has been one of growth and progress.

19

Thompson's Candy

A Sweet Taste of Meriden History

The story of Thompson's Candy is in many ways the story of the American Dream.
—*Ron Robillard, from his book* Sweet Success: A History of Thompson's Candy

The story of Thompson's Candy is intimately linked to the history of Meriden's industrial and commercial evolution. A testament to American ingenuity and entrepreneurial spirit, the company's journey from a modest confectionery cart to a renowned chocolate producer is a captivating saga.

The genesis of Thompson's Candy can be traced back to 1871 when a young William H. Thompson embarked on a quest to master the confectionery trade. His journey led him to Philadelphia, where he apprenticed under the esteemed Stephan Whitman of Whitman Candies, a name synonymous with early American chocolate-making. During his time in Philadelphia, Thompson became an acquaintance of famed chocolatier Milton Hershey. It was during this formative period that Thompson's passion for chocolate was ignited.

Returning to his hometown of Meriden in 1879, Thompson opened the W.H. Thompson Company, a confectionery that offered a range of candies and treats and, by 1881, ice cream. However, his heart lay in chocolate-making. Driven by a commitment to quality and purity, Thompson was determined to create confections free from artificial

additives, an innovative approach during the nineteenth century. It would be this unwavering dedication that set the foundation for a brand synonymous with excellence.

According to the 1880 Meriden City Directory, thirteen dealers, including Thompson, were placed under the heading of *Confectionery and Fruit*; however, several of these businesses were either growers or produce men who may have also carried a side business. Of these, Thompson proved successful. By 1895, the success of his business allowed Thompson to undertake his first major remodeling of his store, something he would do often throughout his lifetime; and in 1900, Thompson purchased a large home for his family in the lovely middle-class neighborhood of Randolph Avenue in Meriden.

As the twentieth century dawned, Thompson's Candy continued to carve a niche for itself. A pivotal moment arrived during World War I when the company received a substantial order for chocolate soldiers from Schrafft's Candy, a Boston-based confectionery giant. This contract propelled Thompson's into the national spotlight, expanding its distribution network and, more importantly, solidifying its reputation as a reliable and innovative chocolate producer.

Before long, Thompson had accounts from Maine to Washington, D.C. But in 1921, during a time of transition, he decided to close the

Opposite: William Thompson used this one-horse wagon to deliver ice cream, an important sideline in the early days of business, to the homes in Meriden. *Author's collection.*

Above: Thompson's Candy, a major manufacturer of chocolate novelties, traces its roots to this Meriden storefront at 76 West Main Street. *Author's collection.*

ice cream business and incorporate under the name of W.H. Thompson Company. Once again, the company prospered and held steadfast as one of the area's top confectioners. In the last year of the decade, though, two major setbacks devastated the company. On June 26, William H. Thompson suffered a fatal heart attack in his office. He was seventy-five years old, and he left his business to his son, Charles. The second blow came with the crippling effects from the stock market crash and subsequent Great Depression. Despite posting sales and consumption records that year, the American candy business was not particularly strong, including Thompson's. In the first two years of the Depression alone, more than eight hundred manufacturing confectioners closed their doors forever. Due to the economic strain, Thompson briefly shut down the factory, although his candy-making never stopped. Thompson and his wife, Dorothy, began making chocolates in the garage of their home. By employing a handful of workers, a third generation of Thompsons began working there. Charles's son, George, also joined the business.

Following the Depression years, another chapter unfolded. As president, Charles reestablished the business as the Thompson Candy Company and turned the business's focus exclusively to chocolate, capitalizing on the growing demand for this indulgent treat. The era was marked by a surge in popularity for molded chocolate novelties, and Thompson's proved adept at meeting this trend.

However, with the onset of World War II, there were unprecedented challenges and opportunities that lay ahead for the confectionery industry. Like many American businesses, Thompson's transformed its operations to support the war effort, demonstrating a remarkable capacity for adaptation and patriotism. Recognizing the importance of this essential commodity, Thompson's shifted its production focus to meet the needs of the armed forces. With the nation's attention focused on the war, consumer spending on nonessential items, including candy, declined tremendously. Despite this fact, the war also created new demands, specifically for chocolate, as it became a staple in military rations.

The company's expertise in chocolate manufacturing proved invaluable. Thompson's produced vast quantities of chocolate bars, specifically designed for soldiers to consume in combat conditions. These bars were packed with essential nutrients and calories, thus providing soldiers with the energy needed to endure the rigors of war. Additionally, Thompson's contributed to the production of other chocolate-based products used by the military, such as cocoa powder for hot beverages.

Beyond its direct contributions to the war effort, Thompson's Candy faced challenges associated with wartime rationing. Sugar, a critical ingredient in chocolate production, was subject to strict rationing to ensure adequate supplies for the military and essential civilian needs. The company had to adapt its recipes and production processes to comply with these restrictions while maintaining the quality of its products.

The end of World War II, however, marked a new chapter for Thompson's Candy. As the nation transitioned from a wartime economy to a peacetime one, the company faced both challenges and opportunities. The pent-up demand for consumer goods—including candy—created a favorable market, while the return of soldiers and the subsequent baby boom fueled population growth and increased consumption. The company capitalized on these trends by expanding its product line and distribution network. It introduced new confections to cater to the evolving tastes of consumers while still maintaining its core line of chocolate products. Additionally, Thompson's Candy invested in modernizing its production facilities to improve efficiency and increase output.

In December 1951, Charles Thompson died, leaving his son as heir to the business. Uninterested in running the company, George Thompson opted for brother-in-law Bill Morrissey to be brought in to help run the business. Morrissey understood that as the demand for chocolate grew, the ability to hand-mold and hand-foil chocolate novelties became challenging. It was he who first introduced automated molding machines to the business in the 1960s, which assisted with the efficiency and production capacity.

Despite the factory's success, Thompson ultimately decided to sell the business. Nearly a century after his grandfather William Thompson began his venture, the company was sold to an outside name. Thompson's Candy was sold in May 1967 to Knowlton White, a Yale-educated mechanical engineer. With much spirit, the White family came in and immediately reestablished the Thompson name as a brand.

One of the most significant milestones arrived in 1973 when Thompson's Candy relocated to its current 114,000-square-foot facility on South Vine Street in Meriden. This new location offered ample space for expanded operations and enabled year-round production, a feat previously hindered by temperature fluctuations in older facilities. This move also marked a turning point, allowing the company to streamline its processes and increase output while maintaining the uncompromising quality standards once established by its founders.

When Knowlton White suffered a stroke in 1978, his sons, Jeff and Allan, stepped up in taking over the business. The elder White was keen on teaching his children early about all facets of the company, including the less desirable jobs. In one six-year period, $3 million in capital improvements were made, and in the first five years, under the White brothers' ownership, revenues increased an amazing 400 percent.

Through the decades, Thompson's Candy has weathered economic storms, changing consumer tastes and industry transformations, yet the company's enduring success can be attributed to its unwavering commitment to tradition, innovation and quality. The brand's iconic foil-wrapped chocolates, including the beloved chocolate marbles and eggs, have become synonymous with festive occasions and cherished treats.

Beyond its commercial achievements, Thompson's Candy continues to play a vital role in the Meriden community. The company has contributed to the city's economic vitality and provided livelihoods for generations of local residents. It currently has ninety employees who work to produce more than two million pounds of chocolate annually. Moreover, Thompson's has been a generous supporter of various community initiatives, reflecting its deep-rooted connection to the city.

Today, Thompson's Candy remains a beloved institution, drawing visitors from far and wide to its factory store. The sweet aroma of chocolate that permeates the air is a testament to the company's enduring legacy. As the world of confectionery evolves, Thompson's continues to adapt while staying true to its core values. The company's history serves as an inspiration, reminding us of the power of passion, perseverance and a commitment to excellence.

20

Meriden's Mighty Three

Silver City Pioneers of Early Baseball

Meriden was always a sports town.

From the fields and stadiums to the uniforms and the statistics, baseball is good design. There's no better evidence of that than the iconic white and red ball. With its pristine white surface and high-contrast red stitching, today's baseball is a beautiful union of form and function, mind and brawn.

The city of Meriden saw the game transform with near-perfect seating. Just a handful of years after organized baseball came into being, Meriden, like so many other small towns along the East Coast, had a hometown team carrying out what would become the country's national pastime.

The 1880s were the first full decade for professional ball, and for Meriden, baseball would yield some of its greatest players from the city's back lots. Although the rules were still changing yearly, the popularity of baseball was a constant. Accordingly, independent leagues were slowly expanding too, such as in Meriden, thus providing a primary training ground for several future major leaguers and three members of the Baseball Hall of Fame.

Minor league baseball made its official debut in the city in 1884, as the local team, the Meriden Resolutes, joined the independent Connecticut State League. In its inaugural season, Meriden finished with a respectable 25-22 record, securing second place in the six-team league. Notably, a young twenty-one-year-old, Connie Mack, born Cornelius McGillicuddy, played for Meriden in 1884, marking the beginning of

Connie Mack, born Cornelius McGillicuddy, was a Major League baseball player and manager who got his start for one season in Meriden with the semiprofessional Meriden Resolutes. *Author's collection.*

his illustrious sixty-five-year career in the sport. Local lawyer and team promoter Cornelius J. Danaher signed Mack as a catcher for a monthly salary of ninety dollars. During that season, Mack hit the only home run at the Meriden ballpark.

Prior to that fabled initial game on April 23, 1884, Waterbury had already won the state championship. But during this particular game, Meriden won by a score of 2–0, a great victory. This win was celebrated with a citywide celebration, a parade accompanied with a band and other manifestations of joy, among them the carrying of brooms by the marchers. Connie Mack was now one of Meriden's own.

Although Mack played only one year in Meriden, he was so well-loved by his fans that upon his departure at the end of the season, they gifted him a gold watch.

For more than half a century, Connie Mack played and managed baseball. His tenure included managing the Philadelphia Athletics for their first fifty years of play, and he was a team owner, or partial owner, for the franchise's entire fifty-four-year existence. He also won nine league pennants and five World Series before his team departed for Kansas City.

Mack's tenure was marked by innovative strategies and an unwavering commitment to player development. However, his influence extended far beyond the diamond. He was a pioneer in encouraging player salary increases, often advocating for fair compensation and laying the groundwork for the modern baseball economy.

In December 1937, thirteen years before he retired as the Athletics manager, Mack was selected for induction into baseball's Hall of Fame. Two years later, in June 1939, Mack was honored at the dedication of the Hall of Fame Museum at Cooperstown. He is remembered as "Mr. Baseball."

It was in Meriden where his baseball journey began, forging a close connection to the city that would endure throughout his lifetime. In fact, many accounts even state that he recalled Meriden as "home," and reciprocally, the city held Connie Mack Day on July 1, 1947, a celebration of his accomplishments in baseball.

On that day, Connie Mack returned to Meriden with his Philadelphia Athletics to play an exhibition game against the local Insilco team at Insilco Field, today's Centennial Plaza. Among the sports notables who attended were "Big Ed" Walsh and Jack Barry, who both made baseball history in Meriden and in the major leagues, and baseball commissioner A.B. "Happy" Chandler. The International Silver Company gave Mack a set of 1847 Rogers Bros. silverware in addition to an engraved tray to each member of the Athletics team. Governor James L. McConaughy represented the state and Mayor Francis R. Danaher the city as the thousands of spectators had an enjoyable time, ultimately raising $5,281.78 in charity for the Meriden Boys Club.

These early games of Meriden were often played over a variety of fields. The north end of Meriden saw ballgames played in the open-space fields that neighbor today's Golden Street. Games were also held in the fields off of Kensington Avenue, a lot already cleared and readied for the Connecticut State Agricultural Fairgrounds. Bradley Park of West Meriden similarly hosted ballgames of a semiprofessional caliber. But it would be a field established just off and east of the present Chamberlain Highway on pastureland known as the "Ten Acre Lot," later simply the Meriden Baseball Park, that the city settled into for its high-status ballgames. The field stood where Pasco and Lockwood Streets and Ames Avenue are today. During the 1880s, the most direct way to the field was by way of Windsor Avenue to Springdale Avenue, although Springdale was unnamed at that time. In fact, Springdale Avenue was nothing more than rocks in the roadway the hearty baseball fans would stumble over going to the games. Those who did not walk to the grounds or go in private carriages may have gotten there in buses or stages for fifteen cents each way. In subsequent years, the grounds at Hanover Park were developed and opened, primarily used by the Meriden Industrial League teams, the Meriden Police team and the Meriden High School baseball and football teams. Meriden public schools used Hanover Park for an annual field day.

The decade of the 1880s was not just about the games and the players. It was also about the community and the fans. The games were community events, bringing together people from all walks of life to

This circa 1886 image depicts Frank Grant of the Buffalo Bisons, a former baseball standout in Meriden. *National Baseball Hall of Fame and Museum.*

cheer for their local team. The Meriden team, with its successes and its star players, brought pride and a sense of community to the people of Meriden.

April 17, 1886, was monumental on many accounts. Newly named the Meriden Silvermen, the city team marked the opening day of the season in the newly developed Ten Acre Lot baseball field. The day also commemorated the birth of the hometown newspaper *Meriden Journal.*

On that day, the grounds were packed with spectators to see Meriden's new team and their visiting opponents from Detroit. The game began at 3:00 p.m. but was over around 4:30. It was only a few minutes after 5:00 p.m. when the newsboys were scampering over the streets yelling out the score with a full account of the game played that afternoon—in this case, the inaugural game in the inaugural newspaper.

Unfortunately, the score was Detroit, 11, and Meriden, 0.

Despite the loss, Meriden welcomed a young Ulysses "Frank" Grant, one of the few Black players who played on the integrated team. Like Mack, Grant was born in Massachusetts during the Civil War and had progressed steadily on the ballfield. Grant began his career as a second baseman and was often referred to as a "slick fielder" with a strong arm who hit for average and had surprising power despite his slight 5'7" frame. This outstanding ballplayer would soon become a local fan favorite, as he was not only exceptionally gifted on the ballfield but also equally humble away from the diamond. Reportedly, Grant was one of six Black players in the otherwise all-white baseball leagues in 1886. In part because of his skill on the field, Grant signed with the Buffalo Bisons in the International League the following year, one level below en route to the major leagues. Unfortunately, the color line was drawn on organized ball the following season, and Grant was forced to play for top-touring Black teams due to the segregation, most notably the Cuban Giants, where he served as team captain and a mentor to younger players.

"Were it not for the fact that he is a colored man, he would, without a doubt, be at the top notch of the records among the finest teams in the country," wrote a contemporary press account on Grant over 130 years ago. He was one of baseball's early stars who became an inspiration for future generations of African American ballplayers.

Frank Grant came back to play in Meriden often, bringing the clubs that he captained. On one such occasion, around the turn of the century, after a game was canceled due to excessive rain, Meriden fans were quite disappointed not to see Grant play in the city where he started professionally.

On one such occasion, both future nineteenth-century Hall of Famers Grant and Mack played against each other. This game was on May 13, 1886, when Grant was with Meriden and Mack was with Hartford in the Eastern League. During the game, Grant put out Mack at second and got an assist on his throw to first on a triple play against Hartford. Grant also stole second and third while Mack was catching.

History will remember Grant as perhaps the greatest of the African American ballplayers who played in organized baseball in the nineteenth century, and despite his lack of major league experience, Grant was inducted into the National Baseball Hall of Fame in Cooperstown, New York, in 2006, as one of the few pre–Negro League players so honored.

"Big" Ed Walsh enjoyed a fourteen-year career in Major League baseball before moving to Meriden, where he worked as a superintendent at the Broad Brook reservoir plant. *From the* Record-Journal.

Years later, during the first quarter of the twentieth century, city baseball continued to produce talented residents such as future Hall of Famer Edward Walsh. Surpassing any such expectations one may have had from an industrial community with a population of then about thirty thousand, Meriden had become a bona fide baseball town that spawned players at the top of their game.

"Big Ed" Walsh was born in Plains, Pennsylvania, in 1881 and came to Meriden to play with the Meriden team in the state league. His first year, 1902, saw him compile a 15-5 record. This mark attracted the attention of Newark of the International League, where he won 9 and lost 3 for that club in the following year. This prompted the Chicago White Sox to buy his contract for $750, then a large amount.

Walsh was a dominant pitcher whose career was cut short by World War I. Known for his devastating screwball, Walsh was a five-time All-Star and a key member of the Chicago White Sox's 1917 World Series championship team. His ability to confound hitters was unparalleled in his era, and his premature departure from the game only heightened the mystique surrounding his talent. Like Mack, Walsh's early ball roots traced back to Meriden, where he honed his pitching skills before ascending to baseball's highest level.

Ed Walsh was elected as a player into the National Baseball Hall of Fame in 1946.

After his big-league days were over, Ed Walsh returned to Meriden and was employed by the city at the Broad Brook filtration plant as its superintendent. He retired from that post in 1953 and died of cancer in Pompano Beach, Florida, some six years later.

Beyond their individual accomplishments, Mack, Grant and Walsh represent a microcosm of baseball history. Mack embodied the managerial genius that shaped the game, Grant symbolized the struggle for equality in a sport that has often been slow to change and Walsh epitomized the pure pitching artistry of a bygone era. Their stories, intertwined with the fabric of Meriden, offer a rich tapestry of baseball lore that continues to captivate fans and historians alike.

As the city of Meriden evolves, it is essential to preserve the legacy of its early baseball heroes. By honoring their contributions and inspiring future generations of athletes, Meriden can solidify its place in the pantheon of American sports history. The city's three Hall of Famers are more than just names on a plaque; they are symbols of a community's passion for baseball and an enduring source of pride for all who call Meriden home. By remembering its baseball past, Meriden celebrates an era of community spirit and a testimony to the enduring power of America's pastime.

21

The Great White Hurricane

The Blizzard of 1888 in Meriden

You don't know what a really big snowstorm is.
—*anonymous*

The winter of 1887–88 would remain etched in the memories of Meriden residents as a time of unparalleled ferocity. The Great Blizzard, also known as the "White Hurricane" or the "Blizzard of '88," was a catastrophic weather event that unleashed its fury on the Northeastern United States March 11–14, 1888. The Great Blizzard of 1888 was one of the most severe blizzards in recorded history and the worst snowstorm in Connecticut's, paralyzing the East Coast from the Chesapeake Bay in the Mid-Atlantic through to Maine.

Unlike more typical winter storms, early forecasts provided little to no warning of the impending disaster. That year, the days of March were warm and spring-like, and the people of Meriden were looking forward to an early summer. It did not seem possible that another snow could be forthcoming, and certainly not one of the largest in many years.

Sunday, March 11, 1888, began as an unseasonably warm day in Connecticut. As the day turned to evening, however, the weather turned colder and a light snow began to fall. Optimistic residents believed that the storm would not last, and many thought it was "just winter breaking up." However, the snow continued to fall into the next day.

By mid-Monday morning, reports from nearby Southington told of a black cloud appearing on the horizon and sweeping over the area. The sky filled with flakes, and visibility declined drastically as temperatures

The Great Blizzard of 1888 was one of the most severe blizzards in history. This photograph was taken on March 12, 1888, looking up Colony Street. *Meriden Historical Society.*

plummeted to fifteen degrees below zero and wind speeds increased. Outside had turned into a raging blizzard. As the wind whipped the snow into a whirling, freezing blanket, it limited one's ability to see only a few feet. People immediately began to leave work or school to return home, but some waited too long and had to wait out the storm from where they were. Some pedestrians even covered their heads with burlap or sacking to keep out the fine, biting snow but allow vision.

On that day, most parents opted to keep their children home from school. The students who did show up, however, were quickly turned away. The only Meriden school that remained open was St. Rose of Lima. About half of the children who had come to the school were picked up shortly thereafter by their parents. With the storm gaining momentum, the remaining half spent Monday night in the parish house.

The snow was fine, and the drifts that formed developed quickly and were quite high. By late Monday afternoon, most of the electric wires were down and the telephones were also out of commission. Many people in the town left lamps burning to light the way for people who might be out, as all of the streetlights were out. Most of the people in town didn't worry about heat because they used coal furnaces in those times.

On Monday evening, Samaritan John Anderson found a man and his horse stranded in a snowdrift. The man had been trying to get home and had gotten lost due to the ferocity of the storm. The conditions outside were so bad that Anderson brought both the man and his horse into his home to give them shelter.

The management of many factories in town realized the difficulties involved in traveling throughout the storm and allowed their personnel to remain in the factories overnight. Streets quickly became impassable. Telegraph and telephone wires were down, and householders were trapped inside for several days.

It snowed steadily until about noon on Tuesday, when it began to subside. Newspaper accounts and personal narratives paint a vivid picture of the blizzard's impact. People huddled together for warmth, resorting to innovative measures to stay alive. Some dug tunnels through the snowdrifts to reach neighbors or access supplies. It was between then and later that afternoon when the storm finally abated and the tunnels were dug. One such tunnel was dug along Main Street completely beneath the snow in order to give the people access to the homes and shops across the street.

Many people thought that by Tuesday evening the end of the snowfall had come, but it began to fall again on Wednesday morning. It snowed steadily until Wednesday evening, when it ended for the last time.

Residents enjoy this big snowbank after the streets of Meriden were opened and sidewalks cleared following the Great Blizzard of 1888. *Meriden Historical Society.*

By now, food and fuel were running short, and some families had neither. Some buildings, such as factories, horse stables or other installations, collapsed under the extreme weight of the buildup of snow. Some factory workers were trapped in their factories for several days. Schools were closed. The only reminder of ordinary life was that some shop owners kept open day and night. In fact, Meriden police ordered store proprietors not to let customers leave their premises.

On Thursday morning, the sun was out and the sky was clear. But Meriden needed to shovel out of the mess; since Monday, the snow had shut the city off from the outside world. In some cases, the snow had reached second-story windows of houses and completely covered some one-story buildings. Children were not allowed outside unless they were in the company of an older, stronger person. Men, in order to get to work, used barrel staves to walk across the snow in place of snowshoes, and in a few cases, they had to dig tunnels to get to their jobs. Neighbors helped neighbors, digging out trapped families and sharing scarce resources. Doctors braved the blizzard to reach the sick and injured. In some towns, citizens banded together to clear roads and establish makeshift shelters.

Great progress was made on Thursday in clearing out from the Great Blizzard. The most spectacular event was the arrival of the first train, the Hartford and Berlin passenger, to the station. Soon thereafter, three more trains arrived, plowing their way from New Haven. Communication between the cities was now reinstituted after an anxious wait of three days.

Meriden, enveloped by mountain ranges to the east and west, suffered more severely than most during the Great Blizzard. The stretch between Yalesville and Meriden was especially bad, particularly in the vicinity of Holt's Hill, present-day Hall Avenue in Meriden. One train coming from the south was stalled there with passengers for two or three days. Among the stranded passengers was an opera company scheduled to appear at the Delavan Opera House in Meriden later that week. The railroad officials later said that the worst drifts in the city were near the Peat Works—today's Beaver's Pond—as they were as high as the top of the smokestack of the nearby icehouse. When it was clear that the railroad needed to reopen, the vice-president of the New York, New Haven and Hartford Railroad ordered up to five thousand shovelers to partake in getting the trains en route from New Haven. Unfortunately, their efforts were fruitless, as the trains were at a standstill.

The end of the week saw business as usual resume in Meriden. The Meriden Brewing Company was out delivering casks all around town. Lyon

The Blizzard of 1888 paralyzed travel in the Northeast. Here, a locomotive engine covered with snow is on railroad tracks beside the Meriden railroad platform. *Author's collection.*

& Billard sold over three hundred baskets of coal, and E.S. Gibbons sold nearly three hundred pairs of rubber boots over the duration of the storm.

The storm, which lasted only three days, dumped over thirty inches of snow on Meriden the first day. Two days later, the total reached over four feet of snow with recorded drifts measuring up to forty feet. In fact, the strong, sustained winds—as high as sixty miles an hour—caused incredible snowdrifts, so much that several families left their homes through a second-story window. More than four hundred people across the East Coast died in the storm, and estimates placed total storm damage at $20 million.

Today's meteorologists agree that two main factors contributed to the large amount of snowfall. The first was the amount of water vapor present in the air, which came from the easterly and northeasterly winds that started in the Atlantic Ocean and then blanketed New England. The second factor was a sudden drop in temperature, which not only made for ideal snow conditions but also added to the already large amount of water vapor in the air.

The Great Blizzard of 1888 brought not only Meriden and Connecticut to a complete standstill but also the entire Northeast. Its significance in Meriden's history remains a demonstration of the power of nature and the resilience of the people who lived through it. Despite the devastation, the people of Meriden faced the storm with humor and heroism, making the best of a challenging situation.

One positive note was that the storm provided an impetus to begin putting utility lines underground. In fact, it was this storm that prompted New York and Boston to begin their subway systems, as many overhead wires broke and presented a hazard to city dwellers and transportation was knocked out for days upon end during this disaster.

The Blizzard of 1888 remains a significant event in Meriden's history. It serves as a stark reminder of the power of nature and the importance of preparedness. Improved forecasting methods, emergency response plans and more robust infrastructure all stem from the lessons learned from that harsh winter. The blizzard also fostered a sense of collective memory, a shared experience that continues to bind communities together. Meriden emerged from the ordeal with a renewed sense of community and a determination to be better prepared for future disasters.

22

A Rustic Retreat

Olmsted's Influence in Hubbard Park

In its natural features Hubbard Park is certainly one of the finest in the country.
—John Charles Olmsted, Frederick Law Olmsted's nephew and adopted son

The idea that Hubbard Park was designed by the great landscape architect Frederick Law Olmsted has been a false claim for decades. Over the years, the idea that he was associated with the design of Hubbard Park has grown considerably.

During the early years of the 1880s, Walter Hubbard, industrialist and Meriden's greatest benefactor, originally spoke of an envisioned public park in the Hanging Hills area of West Meriden. It was to be a serene escape for the people of Meriden. Beginning in 1869 and unbeknown to most, Hubbard began accumulating land around this area at a furious rate. When developments advanced in the planning of this proposed park, however, Hubbard soon realized that he needed professional advice from a park architect.

Hubbard decided to contact Frederick Law Olmsted, the country's foremost trailblazer in landscape architecture. Since Olmsted had already left an indelible mark with his iconic design of New York City's Central Park, for Hubbard, obtaining the artist's expertise was the logical solution.

Although there is truth that Walter Hubbard did, in fact, reach out to Olmsted in the spring of 1898, it was soon learned that Olmsted had retired and was nearing eighty years old. Olmsted did, however, proceed to give the assignment to his nephew and adopted son, John Charles Olmsted,

Walter Hubbard, namesake to Meriden's crown jewel, Hubbard Park, is considered the city's greatest benefactor. *Author's collection.*

of the renowned landscape architecture firm Olmsted Brothers. It would be he who answered Hubbard's invitation and agreed to come to Meriden. He was asked to witness the development of the park and give Hubbard his critiques.

On April 23, 1898, and for one hundred dollars and travel expenses, John Charles Olmsted stepped off a 9:41 a.m. train from Hartford and met Hubbard, who was waiting for him. They headed for the park, where Olmsted would soon meticulously assess its features. After he visited the beautiful woodlands for the day, the firm wrote seven letters to Hubbard between 1898 and 1899 making several recommendations for improving the park. These would include road and walkway design, edge treatments around Mirror Lake and Merimere Reservoir, as well as several improvements to the scenic vistas from the mountain peaks. The Olmsted firm also promoted the building of suitable places within the park to congregate, wrought-iron fencing and the awareness of keeping the park's rustic character, functional and on-site.

Two of these letters were critiques of the development of the park's work thus far, with the second report, dated May 25, 1898, as the most descriptive: "In its natural features Hubbard Park is certainly one of the finest in the country," Olmsted wrote. The peaks are "so beautiful and full of admirable features that we can fill many pages with a description of even the few that have already come under our observation." Olmsted would continue to add that "the rest of the park should be treated in such a way as to preserve as far as possible a natural and rustic effect, or to supply what is lacking to produce such an effect."

John C. Olmsted further emphasized the need to thoroughly adapt the lower and more accessible part of the park for use by the considerable number of visitors, but he also wrote that "the rest of the park should be treated in such a way as to preserve as far as possible a natural and rustic effect, or to supply what is lacking to produce such an effect."

Olmsted further wrote and criticized the practice of Hubbard's allowance of individual landowners to harvest firewood from the hills. He stated that the wholesale cutting of trees over considerable areas created a monotonous landscape and should be avoided. Concerning the trees, Olmsted was strongly of the opinion that the existing woods must be thinned out and large areas should be "grubbed up."

Afterward, although Hubbard did not respond to these letters personally, he did act on some of the firm's suggestions.

Not everything about this collaboration was smooth sailing. Hubbard and Olmsted occasionally clashed over design elements. For instance, by the time of Olmsted's visit, Hubbard had already built the park's first structure, the Hubbard Park Grecian Temple, a key pavilion behind the present-day bandshell. In the letters, the park artist criticizes the construction of this east-end shelter, insisting that the park should be of a rustic architecture and that Hubbard should focus on using local stones for a more natural appearance. Although the pavilion remains today in its original classical state, ultimately Olmsted's vision prevailed, resulting in the remainder of the park's distinctive aesthetic being rustic.

Hubbard's commitment to keeping the park accessible to all was unwavering. He specified that everything related to the park should remain free of charge and cater to the recreation and leisure of the people of Meriden. While the Olmsted Brothers may not have prepared formal plans for Hubbard Park, their influence is also evident in the road and walkway designs that endure to this day.

In April 1898, John Charles Olmsted, nephew and adopted son of famed landscape artist Frederick Law Olmsted, arrived in Meriden to evaluate the park. *Author's collection.*

Once the park was designed, it was still quite hard to build. Loads of materials were carried in and out of the park on carts pulled by horses. The irregular traprock embedded into the earth had to be dug up by hand so that the huge rocks could be pulled out of the ground. Fresh soil was brought in so that trees could be planted, and mazes of waterways and brooks intersected the park. Although roads had to be built throughout the park, Hubbard and Olmsted were in agreement that their design should not interfere with the natural beauty of the park. Hubbard envisioned a nice balance of recreation and nature, and he also wanted to make the park that today bears his name

Prior to John Charles Olmsted's spring 1898 visit to Hubbard Park, the only structure completed was the classical Hubbard Park Grecian Temple. *Author's collection.*

a place of enjoyment for all. He later added playgrounds, an ice-skating area and a variety of playing fields.

Although it was not a Frederick Law Olmsted collaboration as originally planned, Walter Hubbard transformed this vast tract of land into Hubbard Park—a rustic oasis where nature and community converge. Although the Olmsted touch is commemorated in this beloved Meriden gem, it should not be considered a solely Olmsted design. Walter Hubbard's unique forethought prevailed over the majority of the park's development, thus making it a dually designed park.

Today, Hubbard Park stands as evidence of the power of visionary donors and skilled designers working hand in hand to create an enduring public space. And so, Hubbard Park, with its present 1,800-plus acres of commanding height and delightful woodlands, remains in many ways today as Connecticut's greatest park, if not New England's.

23

The Wireless Messenger

A Curious Chapter in the History of Spiritualism

One of the most enduring and perplexing tales to emerge from Meriden's past is that of the Wireless Messenger. In the early twentieth century, a time when radio technology was in its infancy, reports began circulating of disembodied voices heard through these mysteriously cryptic boards. These ethereal messages were often unintelligible, but some claimed to have received ambiguous warnings or premonitions. The most chilling accounts spoke of a disembodied voice, cold and distant, that seemed to emanate from the ether, carrying with it an aura of foreboding. The identity of the Wireless Messenger remains a mystery, with theories ranging from extraterrestrial communication to the hauntings of a troubled soul.

Spiritualism, which had been around for years in Europe, hit America hard in 1848 with the sudden prominence of the Fox sisters of upstate New York. They claimed to receive messages from spirits who rapped on the walls in answer to questions, re-creating this feat of channeling in parlors across the state. Historically, these sisters enjoyed success as mediums for many years; however, by 1888, it had been proclaimed that their act had been a hoax. This, ironically, further increased interest in the spiritualism movement, thus propelling it to grow tenfold in popularity.

The Ouija board later came straight out of the American nineteenth-century obsession with spiritualism. Businessman and attorney Elijah Bond saw this phenomenon as an opportunity to patent the Ouija board and began selling them with planchettes on July 1, 1890, as novelty entertainment items. By February 1891, the first few advertisements had started appearing in papers: "Ouija, the Wonderful Talking Board," boomed a Pittsburgh toy and novelty shop, describing a magical device that answered questions "about the past, present and future with marvelous accuracy" and promised "never-failing amusement and recreation for all the classes," a link "between the known and unknown, the material and immaterial." This fervent fascination with the occult and the afterlife, particularly with those of deceased Civil War relations, increased sales tenfold in America. Talking boards, or Ouija boards as they would later be called, were emblematic of this cultural obsession.

Throughout his lifetime, William Wheeler was a noted mechanical photographer, novelist and inventor of his "Wireless Messenger." *Author's collection.*

This spiritualism boom led Meriden photographer, photo-engraver and businessman William Wheeler to capitalize on his own "wireless messenger." While its physical form—a seemingly ordinary talking board—may appear unremarkable, its historical context and the circumstances surrounding its creation imbue it with an air of mystery and intrigue.

William Wheeler was born in Middlesex County, Connecticut, on January 11, 1853, and came to Meriden to go into business with his brother, Frank. Striking out on his own in 1876, Wheeler became a noted local mechanical photographer in town. However, over the course of his lifetime, he entertained multiple creative endeavors. In 1890, Wheeler made his literary debut as a novelist, with his mystical *Life, A Novel.* He followed with *Rest* two years later and *Slavery, or the Battle of Westfield* in 1895. He is better known specifically for his authorship of spiritualist literature. Wheeler's interest in the metaphysical realm undoubtedly influenced his creation of the Wireless Messenger.

Dated to around 1898, Wheeler's Wireless Messenger is distinguished by its unique design, incorporating features that set it apart from its contemporaries. The incorporation of Wheeler's name and contact information on the board suggests a commercial intent, positioning him as both the creator and marketer of this product. He also advertised two of his books on the backs of these printed boards; conversely, only "Trade

Mark" and "Patents Applied For" was printed on their bottom front side. Unfortunately, trademarks weren't catalogued unless they were registered. Patents, however, were, and on June 14, 1916, William Wheeler received a copyright on the Wireless Messenger.

William Wheeler died on December 27, 1916, just six months after his Wireless Messenger copyright. The man who considered himself a Spiritualist and made a talking board to communicate with the other side crossed over himself shortly thereafter. Coincidentally, his wife, Emma Wheeler, survived her husband by less than a week, passing on January 3, 1917.

Decades later, on clearing out the William Wheeler factory estate at 191 Hanover Street, a great number of Wireless Messengers were found. These were later sold off onto the open antique and collectibles market. Although extremely rare to find for sale, these mystical Meriden relics currently sell at a commanding premium price.

The name Wireless Messenger is intriguing. While the concept of wireless communication was still in its infancy at the time, the name implies a connection to the burgeoning field of telegraphy and radio. This suggests a potential attempt by Wheeler to capitalize on the public's fascination with

The Ouija board came straight out of the American nineteenth-century obsession with spiritualism. This spiritual boom led Meriden businessman William Wheeler to capitalize on his own "Wireless Messenger," shown here. *Meriden Historical Society.*

technological advancement, aligning his product with the spirit of innovation prevalent in the era. However, the Wireless Messenger's significance extends beyond its technological implications. Its existence reflects the broader cultural and historical context of late nineteenth-century America. As a product of the spiritualist movement, it speaks to the profound human desire for connection with the unseen and the yearning for answers to life's ultimate questions. Moreover, the board's design and manufacture offer insights into the production methods and materials of the time, providing a glimpse into the industrial landscape of the era.

24

A Storied Seat of Governance

The History of Meriden's Three Town Halls

But that Meriden Town Hall is as near perfect as perfection can be.
—F.R. Thompson, former builder, said prior to the opening of the reconstructed Meriden Town Hall in 1907

Meriden boasts a rich history intertwined with the evolution of its town halls. Unbeknownst to most, the present-day hall is in fact the third hall to stand on that mark. Each of these structures transcended its role as a mere building, serving as a symbol of civic pride, witnessing pivotal moments and reflecting the changing architectural tastes of a growing community.

Meriden's story as a distinct entity began in 1727 with the construction of a meetinghouse on Meeting House Hill, the present-day corner of Ann Street and Dryden Drive. Although not considered one of Meriden's town halls, this structure should be mentioned; when the community evolved from a parish to a town in 1806, this modest meetinghouse became the first iteration of Meriden's municipal building.

As the nineteenth century witnessed Meriden's transformation into a bustling center of industry, the town's growth spurred the need for a more distinguished town hall. At a town meeting held on April 29, 1844, the movement was started to build a town hall in Meriden. However, it wasn't until nine years later, in 1853, that construction commenced. In the following year, the grand structure in the heart of Meriden, which cost a substantial $60,000, was erected on East Main Street. This impressive building, referred to by residents as the "town house," marked a significant step forward for the town.

This new Meriden Town Hall quickly became a focal point for the community. In 1858, Reverend Henry Ward Beecher, a renowned social reformer, delivered a lecture to a large crowd within its walls. The building achieved even greater historical significance when Abraham Lincoln, then campaigning for president, addressed a packed audience there in 1860. At the time, Meriden's town hall, considered the largest in the state, was a platform for prominent figures and a center for lively public discourse.

Recognizing the growing needs of the town, Meriden embarked on a rebuilding project for its town hall. In October 1888, a committee was formed to oversee the construction of a newly restored city hall. They announced that the city intended to hire a New Haven–based architect to oversee the reconstruction; however, when the public heard about the $10,000 fee, they disapproved and then protested. Two months later, in December, more than two hundred residents came to another meeting, to which the result was a larger committee and an agreement to spend no more than $60,000 on design and construction.

After several presentations from architects from around the state, the committee chose W.R. Briggs of Bridgeport. His plans for the new structure were approved in 1889 and to the voters' liking; the budget was upped to $70,000.

After a few slight delays, construction began, finishing in time for an opening in 1892. The expansion included a clock tower, a central dome and additional space to accommodate the expanding municipal functions, such as a police headquarters with its holding area. It was also earlier decided that the building's design was to resemble Meriden High School, today's Meriden Board of Education building, which stood across the street.

The building, unfortunately, saw tragedy when, on fateful Valentine's Day 1904, disaster struck. That morning, nightwatchman Christopher Wuterich was in the women's cloakroom at about 4:30 a.m. when he thought he smelled smoke. After he called for the Meriden chief, the firemen were quickly summoned. Sadly, the firemen, covered in ice and exhausted after nine hours of firefighting, were unable to save the building, and only the unstable walls remained. It was later deemed that either faulty electrical wiring or a leaky gas jet may have been the cause of the blaze. Fortunately, many of the town and city records remained intact, although they were quite wet from the drenched vault. These documents included city birth certificates, land records and tax records, which were immediately brought across the

Meriden replaced its original town hall with this building, its first city hall, in 1892. It was destroyed by fire on February 14, 1904 (*shown*). *Meriden Historical Society.*

street to the Curtis Memorial Library for the time being. Mayor George S. Seeley moved to a vacant store in the Byxbee block near the post office for a temporary police headquarters, and some city officials were temporarily transferred to office rooms within Meriden's Palace Block. When the fire was initially discovered, Police Captain Charles B. Bowen released the only prisoner in the lockup, a drunk who later insisted on shaking hands with the chief and captain when he learned he was being set free. The blaze not only caused a staggering $130,000 in damages but also injured seven firemen, two of them seriously.

The location of the government building has always been the same, on the parcel of land between Norwood and Liberty Streets along East Main Street; however, there were several discussions over the years about a different plan. After the 1904 fire, officials vehemently debated the site's future. A recurring idea was to develop the site as another city park. Walter Hubbard, a respected local voice and namesake to his recent donation to the city, Hubbard Park, opposed this, as did several others. "Meriden has enough parks," he said. "We should erect a new, modern building without a public hall and put the police into separate headquarters."

The fire that destroyed Meriden's town hall did not dampen the community's spirit. With resolute determination, the town council wasted no time in planning a new house of government. The current Meriden City Hall, built between 1904 and 1907, stands as a testament to this resilience. Although the cornerstone of the current city hall reads 1905, it was completed two years later at a cost of $212,000. No doubt due to its designers' attention to detail and superior materials, today's city hall sports a brick façade with pillars made of limestone from Vermont and is designed in the Neoclassical style. The building also exudes an air of grandeur and permanence. A poignant reminder of the past is etched in a plaque along the northwestern corner of the building commemorating Abraham Lincoln's historic speech at the original town hall.

The current city hall has served Meriden for over a century, witnessing countless events that have shaped the city's trajectory. From the offices of the mayor, clerk and other departments of the city government to the stately Soldier's Monument a short distance to the west of the building, it has been the backdrop for the triumphs and challenges faced by the community. Aside from the customary city official spaces, the present city hall also includes congregating rooms where early town committees met, also used for recreational activities such as dances, bingo and even boxing and wrestling matches.

The evolution of Meriden's town halls is more than just architectural history. It is a narrative of a community's commitment to self-governance and civic engagement. From the humble beginnings on Meeting House Hill to the grandeur of the present city hall, these structures have served as a physical manifestation of Meriden's growth and aspirations. As the city continues to progress, its town halls will undoubtedly continue to play a vital role, standing as silent sentinels to the rich tapestry of Meriden's history.

25

Unveiling the "Meriden Banner"

A Search for a City's 1907 Champion

The City now has its own distinctive emblem to be used on all public occasions.
—*The* Morning Journal-Courier *(New Haven)*

Meriden, nicknamed the Silver City due to its once-booming silver-plating industry, possesses a keen sense of identity. And with that sense of self, a Meriden city seal was established on May 11, 1868. But as the newly incorporated city continued to grow and a transformation from an agricultural economy into a highly urbanized, industrial epicenter ensued, it was decided that a new municipal design was in order.

In 1906, Meriden observed its one hundredth anniversary with a weeklong centennial celebration. With the success of its multiple industries, the city was prompted to create a design for a municipal banner. The Common Council of the City of Meriden made a call to the many and varied industries that had given Meriden its worldwide fame and asked for examples of a distinctive illustration of its skilled trades, which "shall not only be pleasing to the eye but at the same time make an impression upon one's mind." At the time, Meriden was the fifth-largest municipality in the state and one of the finest examples of a flourishing Connecticut town.

This upcoming Meriden banner would be used for a variety of situations, ceremonially as in parades or other city affairs or for such promotions as exhibits at conventions.

Adopted in 1907, this Meriden banner was short-lived. With its sixteen petals, each representing a top Meriden industry, it would be within a few short years that some of these manufactures were lessened and thus the banner discontinued. *Sherwin Borsuk.*

For months, designs of various efforts were proposed. As of 1907, Meriden had ninety-five manufacturing concerns, and to fully render the efforts of these manufacturers into a singular design was quite daunting—that is, until resident Jesse Sands stepped forth with a proposal. It showcased a shield with projecting fronds on which are marked the names of the many varied industries of Meriden: silverware, cutlery, pianos, machinery, spoons, clocks, jewelry, curtains, woolens, casters, hardware, organs, braids, firearms, lamps and glassware. His black-and-white illustration portrays a background bearing a sunflower or an ox-eye daisy. The central circle tells us that it is the municipal banner, and a surrounding circle describes the city as "a merry-den of industries; ninety-five factories." It was accepted without question by the city officials.

On July 1, 1907, a presentation of the handsome silk banner, as the gift of Sands, was made at the meeting of the common council. The presentation was made for the donor by Senator Francis Atwater, and Mayor Thomas L. Reilly formally accepted the emblem.

Senator Francis Atwater remarked at the presentation:

> *It is my pleasure this evening acting for and on behalf of the donor, Jesse Sands, to formally tender and deliver into your keeping this beautiful and instructive banneret, which shall hereafter be known as, the Municipal Banner of the city of Meriden. Its design was explained to your honorable body at its last meeting, when by unanimous vote it was adopted and accepted.*
>
> *Now that it is completed and before you for your inspection I trust it will come up to your expectations, in design, material, workmanship, and artistic beauty, and be cherished as an emblem of civic pride.*

Its purpose is to call attention to the many and varied industries which have given Meriden a world-wide fame; and a distinctive illustration of its skilled trades which shall not only be pleasing to the eye but at the same time make an impression upon the mind. It will do this for the stranger who studies out its import, and also to serve to remind the home resident that he is living in a city whose genius and product are known in every land.

It should not only be displayed on occasions when the city itself entertains, but loaned to citizens, who will properly care for it, for conventions and meetings which may bring it to the attention of those who may visit Meriden at such times.

The information it conveys of the ninety-five factories now here and the variety of goods manufactured may lead the buyer of these lines, if he did not already possess the knowledge before, to inquire if he could not buy better here than elsewhere; if he be a merchant to seek to go into business here in a city wide awake, enterprising and the place to locate; if a skilled mechanic to seek employment, and enjoy the comfort and privileges thousands of workmen now have in this community, and if he seek a location to enter manufacturing the fact that thousands of first-class artisans are now here, he will know from the story that this emblem tells.

The lesson of this banner is to instill into all a feeling of local and civic pride; on all occasions to uphold the fair name of Meriden; to let the world know we have distinctive ideas, and to proclaim that we believe in our own progressiveness and greatness.

Upon final production of the banner for the ceremony, in addition to Sands, due praise was given to Charles S. Palmer, who aided in the design of the banner; Edward D. Bradstreet, who insured the artists' work; and the ladies who did the embroidery and needle work. The whole of the banner was the handiwork of the Meriden people.

As most residents marveled at the banner's skillful encapsulation of Meriden's industrial plain, several Meriden residents felt it wasn't a keen representation. Although the banner indicated some things Meriden had done well to be proud, many residents felt that it was not comprehensive of the Meriden output. What about the homes, the churches, the schools or the traditions? Meriden had much to be recognized. Perhaps Meriden should have been more worthy of a greater, broader and deeply suggestive emblem, thought many.

Despite the mixed feelings, the banner was, indeed, accepted as complete and immediately packaged on the municipal stationery and city flags. The banner even took a commercial route and landed on a set of Meriden-themed postcards. However, it was evident that, over the next few years, although Meriden continued to make rapid strides through the early twentieth century, several noted manufacturers were short-lived and were gone by the First World War. In fact, a great many of Meriden's industries were completely dissolved by the Depression. This ultimately made the Meriden banner an obsolete and incomplete depiction of Meriden's past. It was quickly deemed not practical and discontinued. Today, however, it can be remembered as a memento of a successful and flourishing time in Meriden's illustrious history.

Despite its demise, it remains a great remembrance of what we *were*.

26

The Voice That Captivated a Nation

Rosa Ponselle

The Queen of Queens in all of singing.
—Luciano Pavarotti in reference to Rosa Ponselle

Widely regarded as one of the greatest sopranos of the twentieth century, Rosa Ponselle—born Rosa Ponzillo on January 22, 1897, in Meriden—left an unparalleled mark on the world of opera. The youngest of three children, Ponselle grew up on Springdale Avenue in Meriden, a neighborhood chiefly populated by immigrants from southern Italy. There the Ponzillo family operated a wood and coal business.

Ponselle displayed an exceptionally mature voice at an early age. Despite her early prowess as a piano student, she was more inclined toward instrumental scores rather than vocal music. However, the influence of her older sister, Carmela, who was pursuing a career as a cabaret singer, inspired Rosa to embark on her own stage career singing popular ballads to audiences while working as a silent-movie accompanist.

In 1915, Carmela brought Rosa to audition for her vaudeville agent. Despite being markedly overweight, Rosa impressed with her voice and was hired to perform with Carmela as a sister act. For the next three years, the siblings shared the stage to create the operatic vaudeville acts known as the "Tailored Italian Sisters" and "The Ponzillo Sisters" on the Keith Vaudeville Circuit, earning a substantial income.

While performing in New York, Rosa caught the ear of the legendary opera singer Enrico Caruso, who was deeply impressed with her voice. At his urging, he arranged for Rosa to audition with the Metropolitan Opera Company in New York City. Ponselle was accepted, and on November 15, 1918, at the age of twenty-one, Rosa Ponselle took the stage alongside Caruso in Giuseppe Verdi's *La forza del destino*, marking her debut with the Met. This performance showcased her exceptional talent and cemented her high status. This achievement also paved the way for future American-trained vocalists. In preparing for the role, she studied with Romano Romani, who would remain her principal vocal coach and teacher for the rest of her career.

While Rosa Ponselle possessed a voice of undeniable technical brilliance, it was her artistry that truly set her apart. She possessed a rare ability to inhabit the characters she portrayed, conveying their emotions with a depth that resonated with audiences. Her stage presence was captivating, and her every movement was filled with dramatic purpose. Ponselle was more than just a singer; she was a storyteller, weaving tales of love, loss and redemption through the power of her voice and her acting.

Critics marveled at her vocal range, her effortless control and her ability to imbue characters with depth and nuance. She quickly became a favorite with audiences, particularly later excelling in roles from the Verdi and Puccini repertoire, such as Aida, Tosca and Leonora. Ponselle's performances were hailed for their dramatic power and emotional conviction, transporting audiences to a world of passion, heartbreak and triumph.

Ponselle's operatic journey extended beyond the borders of the United States. She graced London's Covent Garden for three seasons between 1929 and 1931 and delivered three captivating performances of *La vestale* in Florence, Italy, in 1933.

The September 27, 1936 broadcast of *Aida*'s "Ritorna vincitor" is a window into a legendary time when opera was a living, vibrant art form and its audience expected to be profoundly moved by what happened on stage. It was written that "Ponselle was not performing Aida. She was Aida, indeed, desperately torn by the situation she finds herself in. It is impossible not to feel her anguish."

Ponselle worked and worked and worked. There was a lot riding on her shoulders. There had been American stars at the Met before her, sopranos like Geraldine Farrar and Emma Eames, for instance. But they had arrived at the Met after making big careers in Europe. Ponselle was a 100 percent

Rosa Ponselle, often considered to have been one of the greatest sopranos of the twentieth century, poses elegantly in this circa 1920s scene from the opera *Le roi d'Ys*. *Library of Congress.*

product of the United States, homegrown and home-trained. Her enormous success opened the door for other American singers to star at the Met without first going to Europe.

Ponselle's operatic career reached its peak in the 1920s and 1930s. Since her debut at the Metropolitan Opera in 1918, she had spent two sensational decades in leading roles at the Met. During these years, she sang a total of 22 dramatic and dramatic-coloratura roles. She appeared in the leading role of 22 different Met operas and gave 266 performances before retiring from the stage in 1937. This decision stemmed from a quarrel with management, and Ponselle vowed to never set foot in the Metropolitan again.

After she left the company, Ponselle was far from idle. Although she sang only a few live concerts, in 1939, she recorded eight songs for the Victor Talking Machine Company. Sometime later, in 1954, she continued recording, making a number of recordings from her home near Baltimore, known today as the "Villa Pace" soundtracks. It was clear on these recordings her voice was still in remarkable shape. Today, several of these rare recordings of her appearances on radio programs like *The Chesterfield Hour* and the *General Motors Hour* are catalogued and available.

As Rosa Ponselle retired from the opera stage, she transitioned to teaching and mentoring young singers. Her insights and guidance enriched the next generation of vocalists. Ponselle also became the first artistic director of the Baltimore Opera Company. Her passion for opera extended well beyond performing, as she worked tirelessly to promote the art form. Under her leadership, the Baltimore Opera thrived, staging memorable productions and nurturing local talent.

Rosa Ponselle passed away on May 25, 1981, at the age of eighty-four in Baltimore, Maryland. Today, she is remembered through the Rosa Ponselle Foundation. The foundation was established after her passing and continues her mission by supporting young singers and promoting opera education.

Rosa Ponselle's large, opulent voice and expressive ability earned her a place among the greatest sopranos of the past century. Her performances in the title role of Vincenzo Bellini's *Norma* remains one of her most celebrated achievements, just as her interpretation of Norma at the Metropolitan Opera remains legendary. Her chemistry with other cast members, including the Adalgisa of Marion Telva, created magic on stage. Critics praised her for bringing humanity to a character often portrayed as distant and unapproachable. Her voice, a once-in-a-generation instrument, continues to inspire singers and audiences alike. Her dedication to her craft, her commitment to artistic excellence and her dramatic interpretations continue to set a standard for aspiring opera stars. Her story reminds us that greatness knows no boundaries and that the echoes of her voice still resonate through the halls of opera history.

27

Brothers of the Boulevard

The History of the Chamberlain Highway

For many years, Cat Hole Pass in Meriden was a dirt road, nothing more than a bridle path toward neighboring Berlin. But in 1928, the General Assembly approved adding this route to the state's truck highway system. However, the state highway commissioner said that it would likely be twenty years before the state could get to building it. Commissioner John A. MacDonald took notice and conferred with Meriden Mayor Francis T. Maloney, and as a result, the road construction was accelerated. On October 22, 1934, Meriden's L. Suzio Company received the contract for the road on a bid of $256,621.37, and the work was started that fall, financed in part by federal and state funding during the first administration of Frankin D. Roosevelt's New Deal.

A suggestion was later made by Judge James E. Cooper that the new road should be named "Chamberlain Highway" in memory of brothers Judge Valentine B. Chamberlain of New Britain and Governor Abiram Chamberlain of Meriden. These siblings were so devoted to each other that they had made a practice of visiting weekly while they were both alive, using the incomplete road. Ultimately, the road would connect Meriden to New Britain.

Abiram Chamberlain was born in Colebrook, Connecticut, and moved to New Britain, where, at twenty-six, he learned a trade with the Stanley Rule & Level Company. This trade lasted only a short time before he entered the New Britain National Bank, where he worked for a number of years. In 1867, however, Chamberlain came to Meriden as cashier of the Home

National Bank of Meriden. His intimate knowledge of banking and excellent judgment in financial affairs were rewarded with a promotion to president of the Home Bank in 1881. In 1901, he became the state comptroller, serving from 1901 to 1903. In 1903, Abiram was elected governor of Connecticut, an office he had until 1905, the first and, as of this writing, only person from Meriden ever to be elected to that position. Following his years at the capital, he returned to the Home National Bank in Meriden, resuming his role as president of the institution. In addition to his banking connections, he was director of numerous Meriden enterprises and was honored by being made president of the Connecticut Bankers Association and vice-president of the American Bankers Association. Abiram Chamberlain died in 1911.

Judge Valentine B. Chamberlain of New Britain carved out an equally noteworthy career. His gallant record allowed his rise to the rank of captain in the Union army. He was captured by the Confederates in the assault of Fort Wagner, after which he spent time in a Southern prison camp. He was one of the heroes of the well-known war book *The Knightly Soldier*, by Henry Clay Trumbull, which tells of his escape from prison and his recapture just as he was approaching the Union lines. After the war, Chamberlain was editor of one of the newspapers in New Britain, judge of the police court, founder and president of the Mechanics National Bank and treasurer of the State of Connecticut. Chamberlain also became a probate court judge in New Britain and later judge of the city and police courts. He also served as state treasurer while raising ten children, seven boys and three girls. Additionally, Judge Chamberlain was a banker. He was president of the Mechanics National Bank in New Britain up until the time of his death on June 25, 1893, at the age of sixty, more than a dozen years before that of his brother, Abiram.

The first days of August 1935 saw a movement in New Britain begin, with the cooperation of the Meriden Chamber of Commerce, in renaming Cat Hole Pass or Cat Hole Road to Chamberlain Highway. With a formal dedication on the morning of Wednesday, October 9, 1935, both Meriden and New Britain joined in an official opening of the Chamberlain Highway, linking both cities. Charles A. Newton, executive secretary of the Meriden Chamber of Commerce, announced the day as a bugle call opened the festivities, and an opening address delivered by Senator Francis T. Maloney followed. Descendants of both Chamberlain brothers were on hand to greet the crowd.

Prior to Chamberlain Highway, the route called Cat Hole Road probably received its name from the numerous dens that had been inhabited by

On October 9, 1935, dignitaries from both Meriden and New Britain, in addition to members of the Chamberlain family, came out to formally dedicate the newly built Chamberlain Highway. *Allen Weathers.*

wildcats. Also, along this road and up above, the classic profile of the "Father of His Country" George Washington once realistically looked outward from the western-facing peak. Time and erosion took their toll on this formation and have made it difficult to recognize today. In fact, in 1910, park officials were unsuccessful in trying to see if, by artificial means, the likeness could be restored.

The scenic beauty of this highway continues to make it one of the most attractive thoroughfares in the state. It also continues to establish an even more friendly route between the Hardware City and the Silver City, just as it did over a century ago.

28

A Steamy Affair

Unveiling the Origin of the Connecticut Cheeseburger

The world of hamburgers boasts a vast and delicious landscape. From the flame-grilled classics to gourmet creations, each patty tells a story. Nestled in the central Connecticut area lies a unique burger experience: the steamed cheeseburger.

Steamed cheeseburgers are a Connecticut creation with a history going back over one hundred years; however, the exact origin remains shrouded in some debate. Two Connecticut cities—Meriden and Middletown—continue to stake claim to the birth of the steamed cheeseburger, depending on who you talk to. Many believe that it originated from an elderly local street vendor selling portable sandwiches of steam-melted cheese served on a bun. This does seem plausible, but who brought it to the attention of two central Connecticut restaurant owners?

Although both Meriden and Middletown lay claim to the steamed cheeseburger as being their own, one thing is for certain: it has become a central Connecticut food staple. *Author's collection.*

Middletown offered Jack's Lunch, a long-gone restaurant believed to have pioneered the concept in the 1920s or 1930s. Jack's reportedly served steamed cheese sandwiches on rolls, a precursor to the steamed cheeseburger. The story goes that the vendor may have connected

Jack's Lunch hamburger steamer. *Middlesex County Historical Society.*

with Jack Fitzgerald, who, at the age of fifteen, began his career working the lunch wagon scene in Middletown in 1895. Years later, in 1922, when Fitzgerald had gained enough capital to open his own diner, Jack's Lunch, on Main Street in Middletown, he redeveloped a new take on the sandwich he had sold years prior. Fitzgerald's spin on the hamburger, however, was to not grill them, as other eateries did. Instead, Fitzgerald cooked them in a tall copper box and steamed them in a hamburger steamer.

Although Jack Fitzgerald died in 1935, Jack's Lunch continued serving the delicacy for more than three decades afterward, before finally closing its doors in the late 1960s. The restaurant had been in business for forty-four years.

Meriden, on the other hand, also lays claim to a full-fledged steamed cheeseburger variation. Fred Klett is acknowledged to be the first, or at least one of the first, steamed cheeseburger maker in the area. For years, Klett was a staple in the Meriden restaurant scene with his inventive dishes; one such plate, the steamed cheeseburger, would become synonymous with the city. Years later, when Klett eventually sold his Broad Street Diner to Wilson

Veillette, Meriden's longtime tax collector turned restaurant owner, it was decided to keep the famed steamed cheeseburger on the menu.

Meriden's manufacturing was in overdrive due to the war effort of the early 1940s; three shifts were now being instituted among the factories.

Ted's Restaurant, the popular Meriden eatery since 1959, continues to serve its historic steamed cheeseburgers to this day. *Author's collection.*

This meant that Veillette had to keep his steaming cabinet going throughout the evening meal as the call for his steamed hamburgers with or without cheese would continue right through the early morning hours. Among the countermen at the Broad Street Diner was the late Theodore Duberek, who later went into business for himself in 1959 as Ted's Restaurant on Broad Street. Today, Ted's Restaurant is still in business and thriving.

In this tale of two cities, the driving force behind the steamed cheeseburger's invention likely stemmed from practicality. As early twentieth-century Connecticut was an industrial hub, factory workers needed affordable, calorie-dense meals. Steaming, a technique well-suited for mass production, offered a quick and efficient way to cook both the cheese and the patty.

The steamed cheeseburger craze can be traced back to the increased popularity of another local delicacy: the hamburger sandwich. Developed by Louie's Lunch in New Haven around 1900, this ground beef patty between two pieces of bread indirectly helped bring the steamed cheeseburger into the central Connecticut limelight. Another theory suggests that the idea of steaming burgers emerged from the health trends of the time, as steamed food was considered easier to digest than fried food.

However, the enduring popularity of the steamed cheeseburger goes beyond mere practicality. Unlike burgers fried in a pan or grilled, the steamed cheeseburger is prepared in a stainless-steel cabinet containing trays that hold either a hamburger patty or a portion of cheese, which is slowly cooked over boiling water. This steaming method locks in moisture, resulting in a patty renowned for its juiciness. The lack of a sear creates a textural contrast: a soft, yielding patty nestled within a toasted bun. Customary toppings like chopped onions and pickles add freshness and crunch, completing the unique flavor profile.

For over a century, the steamed cheeseburger has remained a cherished tradition in central Connecticut, particularly in Meriden. Local eateries like Ted's Restaurant and K LaMay's continue to carry the torch, offering variations on the classic recipe. While some might miss the smoky char of a grilled patty, the steamed cheeseburger's dedicated fanbase revels in its unique texture and flavor.

Ted's Restaurant, a third-generation family-owned business, has been featured on several media outlets, most notably on the Travel Channel's *Man v. Food*. It also operates a food truck and a concession stand at various locations within central Connecticut. In fact, during the 2018 Minor League

Baseball season, the Hartford Yard Goats played one home game as the "Hartford Steamed Cheeseburgers."

The story of the steamed cheeseburger goes beyond a regional quirk. It exemplifies American ingenuity, where culinary creations arise from a mix of necessity, resourcefulness and a desire for something new. The steamed cheeseburger stands as a testament to the regional variations that enrich the American burger landscape, reminding us that deliciousness can come in unexpected forms.

The steamed cheeseburger's origin story might lack a single definitive birthplace, but its legacy is undeniable. It is a testament to the resourcefulness and culinary innovation that continue to shape American food culture. Whether enjoyed in a classic form or reimagined with new toppings, the steamed cheeseburger remains a delightful reminder that sometimes, the most unexpected methods can lead to the most cherished local treasures. It remains a source of pride and identity for both the people of Meriden and Middletown, whoever may have invented it. As the world continues to evolve, the steamed cheeseburger stands as a reminder of the importance of preserving culinary traditions and celebrating the unique flavors that define a place—and tradition never tasted so good.

29

Meriden's Finest Hour

"The Nation's Ideal War Community"

Meriden was in crisis. The Crash of 1929 and the resulting Great Depression made the prosperity and optimism from preceding decades distant memories in Meriden, let alone the country. One study in 1932 alone concluded that a full 26 percent of the local workforce stood idle, and by March 1938, some 4,048 people had applied for aid from an allotment of available programs and agencies. Some had even lost their homes through foreclosures. However, by the following year, the pressure had begun to lessen in Meriden and funding in the city had begun to be made available. With this and so many federally funded WPA projects allocated to the city, people were on the move.

Overseas, however, a grim story was unfolding. In 1939, the Germans invaded Poland, and World War II began. On the homefront, Meriden was a thriving industrial center, renowned for its silver manufacturing and a hub for a diverse population of skilled workers. With the attack on Pearl Harbor in December 1941, Meriden, like countless other American cities, shifted its focus toward wartime production. Under the municipal leadership of Mayor Francis R. Danaher, the Meriden people joined together to weather these unprecedented challenges. As the community responded immediately to calls for increased manufacturing productivity, they had to submit to the rationing of gasoline, butter and many other goods. Meriden was transformed overnight. The government began buying immense quantities of military supplies and borrowing a lot of money to help pay for them. There were jobs for everybody, and prosperity suddenly returned. With American factories busy turning out tanks, bullets and military uniforms, it was the smaller local manufactories, such as those in Meriden, that supplemented the movement further. Several local businesses soon received government accounts to help America's crusade. These businesses were given federal support to manufacture items. As Meriden business and industry had kept as many of their employees on the payroll as possible throughout the Depression years, the city's major factories had increased their total number of employees now from about 6,500 to almost 11,000. By 1944, more than 80 manufacturing plants in Meriden had accomplished near 100 percent conversion to wartime production needs. The decade of the Depression was over, but a new decade marked by war and destruction was about to begin.

One of the key factors behind Meriden's success was its robust industrial base. Meriden was already home to a diverse range of factories that were asked to produce essential goods for the war effort. When the call to arms sounded, these factories transitioned to support the needs of the nation, working tirelessly to supply the Allied forces with the materials required for victory. The silver-making factories, such as International Silver Company, Meriden's largest employer, began making delicate surgical instruments in addition to gun cartridges and bomb fuses. The lighting fixture factories began making a variety of small-part war articles. The Meriden factories that made telephone sets and ball bearings worked exclusively for the army and navy. Most Meriden enterprises, which prior to the war were in operation mainly nine to five, remodeled their days to three shifts, twenty-four hours a day. The Napier Company began designing and manufacturing war medallions rather than its usual costume jewelry, and the Lacourciere Paint Supply store added a specialized line of "blackout" paint to be used for the U.S. military. This uniquely designed paint was used to camouflage the country's overseas bombers that flew at night. In total, Meriden's industries supplied over 40 percent of the nation's silverware needs, 10 percent of its ammunition and 35 percent of its surgical instruments during the war. This industrial transformation demonstrated the city's adaptability and its commitment to the war effort.

Meriden also excelled in mobilizing its citizens. Civilian defense organizations like the Meriden War Council and the Women's Volunteer Corps coordinated scrap metal drives, collected blood donations and organized entertainment for troops stationed nearby. Victory gardens sprouted in backyards, supplementing the national food supply. The city's residents, young and old, men and women, all contributed in some way, fostering a sense of shared purpose and unwavering patriotism.

Underlying all of these trials and tribulations was a citywide spirit and commitment that would result, in part, in Meriden being selected as the "Nation's Ideal War Community."

The awarding of the title was marked by a ceremony that celebrated Meriden's contributions to the war effort. Previously, the California-based media production company Metro-Goldwyn-Mayer had joined with the U.S. Manpower Commission to produce a motion picture titled *Main Street Today*. This film was uniquely designed to be a morale builder for the war and to be shown all over the country. On March 21, 1944, Paul McNutt, war manpower commissioner, along with other high-ranking federal, state and local officials, addressed the nation in a radio broadcast from Loew's Palace Theatre in Meriden prior to the movie's national debut. Notable entertainers of the time, including Meriden's Walt Solek Orchestra and Captain Glenn Miller's AAFTTC band from Yale University, played; movie stars Luise Rainer, Jimmy Durante, Louise

In a special ceremony in celebration of International Silver's support during World War II, Admiral Wat Tyler Cluverius speaks to the crowd as Senator Francis Maloney looks on. *Meriden Historical Society.*

Allbritton and Lucy Monroe spoke briefly, too, as they had done earlier in the day at a luncheon for five hundred, served in the new cafeteria building of the New Departure plant.

As announced to the city by Chairman Paul V. McNutt of the War Manpower Commission:

> *This community is a perfect example of how the Main streets of America have completely mobilized every resource for war.... The people of Meriden are making their contribution and that means management, labor, city officials, housewives, students, and returning veterans of World War Two. Meriden is solving its own Manpower problems in the best democratic tradition of this nation.*

The benefit of the people of Meriden functioning during an incredible war effort could be seen immediately. The change was accomplished thanks to the spirit of cooperation, which, deeply acquired in normal times, had made this area the greatest and most powerful producer in the country. In addition to the city's national title, several area factories were later recognized and awarded for their wartime cooperation and output.

In an effort to obtain an overall picture of industrial war problems found in manufacturing cities, 161 days after the announcement of Meriden's title, Vice President Henry A. Wallace made an unexpected visit to Meriden. During his time there, he discussed with Meriden Mayor Francis Danaher the status of many industrial concerns, as well as aspects of the peacetime employment situation that might be expected in local industries when civilian production is resumed.

The Meriden population had grown to about forty-six thousand by 1944, and of this number, about twenty thousand were engaged in war-related work and half of them were women. More than five thousand Meriden men and women served in the armed forces during the war years. It was said that the city had the esteem of proclaiming one out of ten persons, be it man or woman, wearing a military outfit, and of every three persons, one worked in a factory producing war goods.

The designation of an Ideal War Community was not solely due to industrial output. It was also a recognition of the community's spirit and sacrifice. The citizens of Meriden rallied to support the war effort, embodying the patriotic spirit that defined the American homefront. From bond drives to volunteer work, the people of Meriden contributed in every way possible, demonstrating a united front against the Axis powers. Meriden could also be proud of its smoothly functioning civilian defense organizations, with thousands who were enrolled to take up emergency duties in case of enemy action. Many of the city volunteers had received hundreds of hours of instruction and practice.

Just about everyone else left at home, including the city's retired, pitched in to do what they could: filling in for those in the service, manning the United Service Organization located in the YMCA building on West Main Street, collecting scrap metal, saving stamps and organizing bond drives.

The story of Meriden's wartime contributions isn't without its complexities. While the focus has often been on industrial production and civilian mobilization efforts, the experiences of minority groups and those who opposed the war deserve acknowledgement. The wartime boom masked racial tensions within the factories, and the unwavering patriotism could have ostracized those with pacifist views.

However, when the war ended in 1945 and the city veterans had returned home, they found themselves on the doorstep of a hometown different from the one they left behind. Meriden had matured greatly. It was then that the Meriden factories converted back to making peacetime goods. Subsequently, with war recovery on a firm basis and the increase of industry humming as far as Meriden was concerned, the city had busy and prosperous following years in 1946 and 1947.

Meriden's selection as the Nation's Ideal War Community during World War II was a significant chapter in the city's history. It highlighted the critical role that Meriden, as an American city, and its inhabitants played in supporting the war effort. Today, this recognition stands as evidence of the city's resilience and commitment to the greater good. It is a legacy that continues to inspire pride among residents and serves as a reminder of the power of community in times of need. Meriden's story is one of unity, determination and patriotism—a narrative that resonates with the enduring spirit of the American people. The title, while acknowledging the city's achievements, also prompts reflection on the complexities of war and the experiences of all residents during this challenging time.

30

Meriden's Golden Legacy

How a Flower Sprouted a Festival

I sincerely feel that your idea could become a reality.
—Frederick C. Mandeville, former Meriden Parks and Recreation director, to Carter White, Meriden Record *newspaper publisher, on the idea of beginning an annual daffodil festival in Meriden*

The vibrant yellow blooms of daffodils have become synonymous with spring in Meriden. These cheerful flowers grace parks, gardens and personal yards, blanketing the city in a dazzling display of color. But the story of daffodils in Meriden goes well beyond mere aesthetics. It's a narrative interwoven with civic pride, community spirit and a unique celebration that has become a cherished tradition.

After World War II, Meriden was in good shape. In March 1944, Meriden had received the designation of Nation's Ideal War Community from the U.S. War Manpower Commission, a recognition of its industrial and patriotic contributions. Despite the world crisis at the time, this moniker had a profound effect on the city's public morale. On a municipal level, the city was on an upswing with improvements, including Meriden's park system. James J. Barry was the city's superintendent of parks, a title earned after beginning with the Meriden Parks Department as a laborer as far back as 1933 and later being promoted to the chief position eight years later in 1941. It was Barry who would, as Meriden history would come to remember, be responsible for the daffodil craze in the city.

On the other side of the world, in northern Europe, the Netherlands faced challenges both during and after the war. In Holland, during World War II, food became scarce. The Germans were deeply involved in northern Europe, especially in Holland, and had commandeered most of their food supply. In order to meet their adequate nourishment, the Dutch began eating flower bulbs. Since Holland raises flower bulbs to sell all over the world, there were plenty of these on hand. They had hoped that they would be able to digest daffodils, a plant that they had an ample supply of, but instead, they got very sick. They did notice, however, that their bodies could tolerate the tulips, which they ate. By the end of the war, the poor and sickened country relied on its major source of income—selling bulbs—to generate revenue. The Dutch, emerging from World War II with resilience, began focusing on their agriculture, recovery and international bulb exports. This revitalization also included sending flower-selling salespeople to the United States to restart their economy, and it was one of these salesmen who introduced Meriden to the idea of daffodils in the park.

James. J. Barry had been appointed to superintendent of parks after his predecessor Donald Robison's untimely death while serving in World War II. Both men had innate concerns for the landscape and beautification of the Meriden parks, specifically Hubbard Park.

Barry, along with his wife and two children, resided in the quaint stone house most commonly remembered as the Hubbard Park Caretaker's Home, which is located on the eastern edge of the park. It was there one evening in the fall of 1948 that a Dutch salesman approached the home, eager to sell the foreign flower bulbs to the city park superintendent. Although Barry did have minimal interest in the purchase, he dismissed the salesman and politely declined. Unable to accept his decision, the salesman repeated his pitch; Barry, perhaps now slightly irritated, motioned to the salesman to meet him across the street at the local basement tavern, Rathskeller. Barry, along with his son, James Jr., met the seller.

There, the meeting was likely short. The salesman, courteous and in hopes of a sale, entertained the uninterested Barrys, who were eager to get back. At last, however, they struck a deal—a deal for one thousand daffodils.

As the Barrys headed back through the park, the younger, taking charge of the bulbs, asked his father where he wanted the flowers to be planted. Without hesitation, the still-uninterested elder motioned to the park's north woods and simply said to unload them there, which the younger Barry did.

The daffodil bulbs were forgotten. That is, until the following spring, when parkgoers were treated to a brilliant display—a stunning patch of bright daffodils—along the tree line. The accomplishment of Barry's previous year's acquisition drew much attention and praise that spawned increased daffodil purchases for Meriden over the next several years.

With each passing year, Barry promoted the yellow flowers as the city's first official sign of spring. This intensified until the spectacle, four years later, caught the attention of Mayor William J. Cahill. On April 19, 1953, he, along with Barry, created Meriden's first Daffodil Day, a celebration with over 150,000 of the bright yellow flowers along the shores of Mirror Lake and in the park's woods. Mayor Cahill also issued the first Daffodil Day proclamation on that day, making it the city's official flower. Meriden was yet to find that, decades later, this event would become the impetus to an annual

James J. Barry's storied forty-year tenure as the Meriden superintendent of parks began in 1941 and lasted until his retirement in 1972. *James J. Barry Jr.*

weekend event designed to attract attention to the hundreds of thousands of daffodil blooms on display in the park.

For years, the annual daffodil bloom remained a reminder that spring was in the air. By 1970, there were eighty thousand daffodil plants of fifty-one varieties in bloom in Hubbard Park. It was also that year that Meriden's Mayor Donald T. Dorsey dubbed the last Saturday and Sunday in April "Daffodil Weekend." He continued to say that this should be a forerunner to yearly open-air daffodil festivals in Meriden. Although the mayor's suggestion brought support from the chamber of commerce and the city's beautification committee, the festival he envisioned was still a few years away.

Throughout the 1970s, Meriden's reputation as a "daffodil city" was well established, and the idea of a daffodil celebration remained on the minds of many, often recurring in local newspaper editorials and the like. Thoughts such as, "it would be a good way to welcome spring," or "it would be a good way to promote Meriden," and "it would be a good way to make Meriden more attractive," were all comments to procure an annual daffodil celebration. But still, there was no action.

Meriden needed a celebration to call its own.

While the flower festivity was sidelined for the time being, Meriden resident and INSILCO advertising director Robert Treloar, and later, Assistant Director of the Meriden Parks and Recreation Mark Zebora, among several others, organized a local downtown extravaganza in response to the 1976 Bicentennial, the Meriden Expo. This celebration was held on Labor Day weekend and brought about 150,000 people to the city's downtown over three days. Although quite successful, it was short-lived. The initial success of the Expo began to subside just a couple years later, and it ultimately ended in 1981 due to a diminished size and low profits. This closure propelled even more increased local interest in reviving the Daffodil Weekend as an annual festival in Hubbard Park.

In a March 1978 letter, *Record-Journal* publisher Carter White proposed to Mayor Walter Evilia that the city transform "Daffodil Day" into something a bit more. "Hubbard Park has without doubt the best displays of daffodils every spring of any city or park in the state," White wrote. "We have lots to be proud of in Meriden, and the Hubbard Park daffodils are one of the most striking examples. It would do credit to your administration to start such a permanent program."

Parks Director Frederick C. Mandeville replied to White on behalf of the city, "I sincerely feel that your idea could become a reality."

DEPARTMENT OF PARKS AND RECREATION

460 LIBERTY STREET April 11, 1978

Mr. Carter H. White, Publisher
Meriden Record Company
Crown Street Square
Meriden, Conn. 06450

Dear Carter:

As per your letter to Mayor Evilia, please be advised that the idea of Meriden becoming the Daffodil Center of Connecticut is one that previous Park and Recreation Commissions along with Mr. James Barry, former Superintendent of Parks, have had.

I have taken the liberty to enclose a copy of a memorandum to Mayor Evilia, dated March 16, 1978, and I sincerely feel that your idea could become a reality and the proposed committee could be formalized.

Very truly yours,

Fred

Frederick C. Mandeville, Director
Parks and Recre tion Department

FCM:ml

Enc.
cc: Mayor W.Evilia

Above: In this April 11, 1978 letter, Meriden Parks and Recreation Director Frederick C. Mandeville replies to *Record-Journal* publisher Carter White's suggestion for the city to transform its "Daffodil Day" into a more elaborate community event, one that would later become the Meriden Daffodil Festival. From the *Record-Journal*.

Opposite: In 1978, this small group of volunteers put forth a four-hour celebratory picnic acknowledging Meriden's yearly daffodil bloom. This quaint celebration was considered Meriden's first Daffodil Festival. *Author's collection.*

In 1978, a small group of volunteers with a budget of $635 in donations put on a four-hour picnic. This event would later be considered the first Daffodil Festival. Credit deserves to go to the first Daffodil Festival committee. Chaired by Kathy Olson, a Meriden public school teacher, its members included Mark Zebora, then acting city superintendent of parks; Thomas Potter, school art director; Mayor Walter Evilia; Eileen Hayes of the beautification committee; Barbara Barillaro, representing the Potpourri Garden Club: Elenor Brenner of Citizens for Meriden; and Peter L'Heureux of the Greater Meriden Chamber of Commerce. These and others, such as Mandeville and the late Carter White, publisher of the *Meriden Record-Journal*, helped manifest the celebration.

That year, Mayor Walter Evilia encouraged Director Frederick C. Mandeville to appoint a committee to help the festival grow.

Between 400,000 and 500,000 daffodils were in full bloom as Meriden welcomed the opening of the celebration of Daffodil Week in April 1979. The group also hosted the first Little Miss Daffodil pageant as part of the festival. Six-year-old Heather Young was chosen as the first "Little Miss Daffodil" in front of about two hundred people in a rain-soaked Hubbard Park. In a brief ceremony, Mayor Walter Evilia also drew the name of Kathleen LeVasseur to be "Daffodil Week's Senior Citizen." While rain dampened the beginning of Daffodil Week in Meriden, the weather held out for the culminating parade.

According to a Meriden newspaper article, Chairperson Olson predicted correctly: "Daffodil Week now and in years to come will be a growing tourist attraction. Meriden's central location and easy access will help in promotion combining both aesthetic and financial appeal."

By 1980, the committee's budget had swelled to $2,000, bringing more people to the picnic at the park.

Overwhelmed by the amount of work, the volunteers turned control of the festival back over to the city in 1982, according to newspaper accounts. But in 1985, with the resurrection of the Daffodil Festival committee, the festival's continued growth was put into motion. The following year, the committee pitched the Silver Fork Food Tent, and thirteen of the city's nonprofit groups gathered to serve food and raise funds for themselves. The same year, a dinner and fireworks display marked the rededication of Castle Craig Tower. The festival was once again a grand Meriden celebration.

In the late 1980s, the Daffodil Festival continued to flourish. A pageant was expanded into a citywide contest that included participation from each Meriden elementary school, and with time came a craft fair and citywide tag sale. According to the *Meriden Record-Journal*, in 1995, about eight thousand people flooded the park for the festival; by 1997, just two years later, the number of attendees had shot up to thirty thousand.

Despite the park's continued success over the years, March 2020 saw the unthinkable as the park's mainstay festival was canceled for fear of risking visitors in the coronavirus pandemic. During this time, park access was strongly limited; after a hiatus, the 2022 Daffodil Festival returned with a bang—welcoming record-breaking crowds.

The next few years saw additional changes. Fluctuations in weather patterns proved a hindrance, hampering peak bloom times and soaking the festival attendees in rain, thus sparking the Daffodil Committee, in 2024, to shift the festival to the first week in May rather than the customary last weekend in April. Additionally, economic downturns necessitated adjustments to festival programming. With each of these alterations, the festival's core spirit remained steadfast. Dedicated volunteers and city officials continually strive to improve and adapt the event.

Daffodils continue to hold a special significance in Meriden. They symbolize the arrival of spring and are celebrated with the annual festival, a tradition for over four decades and one of Connecticut's most beloved events. It remains a two-day event that brings thousands of people to the city each spring. Attractions such as carnival rides, food trucks, a craft fair and an amazing fireworks show are all set against more than 600,000 beautiful daffodils as their backdrop. Locals and visitors alike gather to revel in the sea of yellow blooms, music and festivities. One thing that deliberately hasn't changed is the festival's free admission and free parking.

From humble beginnings in public parks to a vibrant festival and a citywide symbol, the story of daffodils in Meriden is one of community spirit, resilience and a love for nature. The annual festival continues to attract visitors from across the region, solidifying Meriden's reputation as a "daffodil destination." As future generations plant, nurture and celebrate these golden blooms, the legacy of the daffodil in Meriden is secured, ensuring a joyful springtime tradition for years to come.

31

Vincent Lamberti

The Chemist Behind the Iconic Dove Beauty Bar

For many years, Meriden was the home to Vincent Lamberti, the chemist who played a pivotal role in the development of a revolutionary product—Dove soap.

The youngest son of immigrants from Avellino, Italy, Vincent Lamberti was born in 1928 and grew up in Meriden. As a child, Lamberti could be seen frolicking in his parents' grocery establishment, Lamberti's Grocery Store, on Hanover Street during the years following the Depression. In his teens, Lamberti began a plan that would direct his future. Science quickly took hold, as his first love was astronomy. He had aspirations of being an astrophysicist, and this mindset quickly prioritized his studies. In fact, in his later teenage years, Lamberti was so intellectual that he substitute-taught his high school physics class whenever the teacher was absent.

While attending Meriden High School, Lamberti found interest in chemistry, a discipline in which he would remain. He won a prestigious scholarship to Yale University. In high school, he also met his future wife, Ileana. However, it wouldn't be until a blind date sometime later, with Vincent then at Yale and Illeana an English literature student at Harvard, that they began their courtship.

Lamberti earned his undergraduate degree in 1947 and eventually earned his doctorate in organic chemistry in 1951. While attending Yale, he was also a member of Phi Beta Kappa and the Sigma Xi society.

After interviewing with major drug and chemical companies, his career path began at Lever Brothers, a major soap manufacturer, in 1949. It was here that he would spend his career and stay for over forty years.

Meriden native Vincent Lamberti of Lever Brothers, later Unilever, is credited with overseeing the invention of several common household items, including Dove soap. *Meriden Historical Society.*

Established in 1883, Lever Brothers was already a major player in the soap industry by the time Lamberti joined. Its most famous product at the time was Lifebuoy, a disinfectant soap marketed for its cleanliness. However, Lamberti's role at Lever Brothers was multifaceted. He served as both patent coordinator and manager of organic chemistry. The former role involved overseeing the intellectual property generated by the company's researchers, ensuring their discoveries were protected. As manager of organic chemistry, Lamberti led a team dedicated to exploring the potential of organic compounds in various applications, including personal care products. There, his expertise and innovative spirit came to the forefront.

The mid-twentieth century saw a growing consumer demand for milder and more skin-friendly alternatives to traditional bar soaps. These soaps, often made with animal fats, could be harsh and drying. Lamberti and his team spearheaded the development and embarked on a quest to develop a gentler cleansing bar. Lamberti identified a streamlined and relatively inexpensive process to manufacture a synthetic compound to replace the fatty acids in bar soap. He proudly secured his first patent. It was for a low-suds liquid clothes washing detergent marketed as Hum. Ever-tweaking compounds based on demand, he also later developed a high-suds version of dishwashing soap. This breakthrough paved the way for Dove soap, a milder and gentler alternative to traditional bar soaps.

Dove soap's launch in the 1950s marked a turning point in the personal care industry. Lamberti's invention offered consumers a gentler alternative to existing cleansers, and the brand quickly gained popularity. Dove became a global phenomenon, offering a wide range of beauty and personal care products that emphasize gentle cleansing and nourishment for the skin.

Beyond Dove soap, Lamberti's influence extended further. Several of his other patents never made it to the production line, but there are a number that continue to grace the aisles of today's supermarkets and are in the homes of many. In fact, Lamberti developed common household items many take for granted. In addition to a soap made without animal fat named Dove, he formulated a gel toothpaste called Aim, a cheap and satisfying pancake syrup called Mrs. Butterworth's and a household laundry detergent named Wisk. Each of these was concocted with Lamberti's hand.

Although his life was dedicated to scientific exploration and discovery, in this line of work, animals are often used in the testing of products. Lamberti was an opponent of animal testing and did not actively participate in that practice. As imagined, this antagonized several conversations over the years, and Lamberti's one misgiving was that products he had a hand in were tested on rabbits.

Lamberti carried quite an unusually robust portfolio of granted patents. Aside from his 118 credited with Unilever in the United States alone, there were a number of others throughout the world. Records suggest he collectively authored over 2,000 patents for other inventors. This dedication to scientific progress and fostering innovation speaks volumes about his character. Years later, due to a fire in the home, an additional hundreds of unrealized patents were set ablaze.

He was featured on the cover of the *New York Times* magazine as one of America's outstanding young scientists.

Vincent Lamberti died on March 21, 2014, after a series of complications from congestive heart failure in New Jersey, but his legacy lives on in every bar of Dove soap sold around the world. His dedication to scientific exploration and his focus on consumer needs resulted in a product that continues to be a favorite for millions. Lamberti's story is one of innovation and the enduring effect that a single invention can have on everyday lives.

Vincent Lamberti's role in the world of personal care is undeniable. His invention of Dove soap revolutionized the industry, offering consumers a gentler and more skin-friendly cleansing experience. Lamberti's dedication to scientific exploration serves as an inspiration for future generations of scientists and product developers. While best known for the iconic Dove Beauty Bar, his legacy extends far beyond this single product, encompassing a lifetime of scientific inquiry and innovation.

32

The City Charter and the City Manager

A Blueprint for Governance

If it weren't for the 1970s, the new city charter with its city manager form of government never would have been constructed and approved.
—Meriden Morning Record and Journal *newspaper editorial, January 2, 1980*

At the heart of Meriden's municipal structure lies the city charter—a foundational document that outlines the framework for governance. The charter defines the roles, responsibilities and powers of local government entities, ensuring efficient administration and accountability.

Once Meriden received its city charter in 1867, its first order of business was the election of a mayor and other officials to oversee the city's almost nine thousand residents. The voters overwhelmingly selected Charles Parker as Meriden's first mayor. Not unlike today, he and his administration immediately confronted issues such as the provision of water resources, the need for a sewer system, paved streets, police and fire protection, the establishment of new tax rates and the writing of a municipal code. It was not until 1870 that the first arrangement of Meriden's by-laws and amendments to the 1867 charter was recorded. Since that time, numerous changes, additions and deletions have occurred. The year 1979 would prove one of the most controversial.

Historically, the city's mayor served one-year terms, but in the twentieth century, the term was extended to two years. With the adoption of a new city charter in 1979, Meriden's government would be conducted by a city manager, responsible for the day-to-day operation of the various municipal departments and agencies. The Court of Common Council, today simply known as the City Council, was responsible for policy-making and legislation. At least that was the theory behind the charter changes. As the 1980s approached, the theory and application of the newly adopted city government sometimes turned out a bit different.

All of Meriden's mayors, whether popularly elected or elected by the majority party on the council, have made contributions to the city's development. Most of the time, these contributions were positive; sometimes they were not.

On January 3, 1972, Abraham G. Grossman took office as Meriden's mayor after narrowly defeating the incumbent, Robert A. Schultz, in a fiercely contested election the previous November. Grossman served two terms, first from 1972 to 1973 and later from 1976 to 1977, and each would be marked by solid city advancements on one hand and some controversial actions on the other. All the while, however, Grossman remained a "people's" person. He knew how to shake hands and converse with the townsfolk, and more so, he was a successful business owner in the city as the proprietor of Grossman's Shoe Store on West Main Street.

During his term, Grossman made several notable contributions to Meriden, such as expanding recreational facilities by acquiring Nessing Field on Murdock Avenue, enhancing the street surfacing program, improving the storm-sewer network and phasing out the urban renewal agency.

However, Grossman also faced significant challenges. Throughout his early years as mayor, West Main and Colony Streets saw a wave of long-established businesses closing or relocating. Notable enterprises such as Kassabian's Furniture, Besse-Boynton's, Jupiter's, Howland's Styletex Company, Colonial Bank and the Swift Meat Company either shut down or moved to the newly built Meriden Square. This exodus left Meriden's central business district with only a few retail establishments, and Grossman was partly blamed for the downtown's decline.

Unsettled council meetings and one-sided decisions made by Grossman eventually prompted a majority vote by the council in September 1972 to censure the mayor. Unscathed, Grossman went about his business and continued in his old ways, much to the concern of the aldermen. Meanwhile, Grossman oversaw the construction of the Jefferson Savings

Abe Grossman was a prominent figure in the history of Meriden politics. He would be later known as the catalyst for the shift from a popularly elected mayor to a city manager form of local government. *From the* Record-Journal.

and Loan Association building on Colony and West Main Streets and laid the groundwork for Hanover Towers.

This was the first time in Meriden's history that such action was taken. The censure was approved due to the mayor's failure to cooperate with the city charter's provision for a strong council–weak mayor form of government. Despite his progressive city developments, Grossman continued to receive negative reactions from the public.

Grossman managed to embroil himself in virtually every important meeting, often confusing committee members and creating chaos among city employees. In 1972, in a fit of anger, he fired the entire tax board, charging them with "dereliction of duty." Most of them eventually returned, but a few stayed away, taking personal offense at the mayor's actions.

He continued steadfast and weathered the remaining year of his first term. When he went into office, the people of Meriden saw a distinct change in his power and authority.

Grossman's administration did, however, render several notable achievements, such as the approval of an industrial park on Pomeroy Avenue; the opening of the new Meriden Public Library in June 1973; and the continued growth of condominium and planned residential developments for Meetinghouse Village, Mattabasset and Sterling. Additionally, the Meriden Redevelopment Agency was dissolved, a new firehouse site was approved for Capital Avenue and plans for the Miller Memorial Community were announced.

In 1973, the Republicans saw an opportunity to capitalize on the tumultuous Grossman years and nominated John Quine.

Grossman's first turbulent term ended with a municipal election that saw him defeated by John D. Quine, a local printer. With Quine's election, the city's primary concern was to stabilize the situation that had been stirred up during the final months of Grossman's administration. Quine's tenure marked the beginning of the end of a phase in Meriden's political history, as growing popular sentiment supported changes to the city charter, with officials and the public alike questioning the city's governance.

Like previous administrations, Quine faced challenges due to an unfavorable employment situation in the area. Although the city was set to receive over $3.6 million in the next five years from the Federal Housing and Community Development Act, economic uncertainty stalled commercial development. Despite this, housing for low-income and elderly residents increased with the opening of the Harbor Brook Apartments on July 19, 1975, and additional apartment and family housing projects were completed in the central downtown area.

Toward the end of Quine's term, he imposed a mini-tax on Meriden, which ultimately led to his political downfall. Grossman, eager for a comeback, seized this opportunity. As the 1975 municipal election approached, the former mayor set his sights on running again. He convinced the Democratic Party that he was a "changed man" and secured their endorsement. Grossman won the mayoral seat for a second time, defeating Quine in the election. However, even before his second term ended in 1977, Grossman had once again provoked the city council.

On November 17, 1976, in a front-page editorial in the *Meriden Record* titled "The Last Straw," Carter H. White, the publisher of the local newspaper, called for Abe Grossman's resignation, accusing him of fraudulently signing an application for federal funds without consulting the City Council.

Abraham Grossman's second term seemed to mirror his first in many ways. Despite his volatile nature behind closed doors and during council meetings, Grossman continued to advance the city's infrastructure and support its residents.

However, in 1977, armed with a ruling from Corporation Counsel James M.S. Ullman, the Meriden Democrats on the council attempted to impeach Grossman and officially censured him once again. This time, they charged him with fifty-one counts, primarily criticizing his inability to properly administer several city affairs. These included his takeover as an administrator of the Housing and Community Development Act, which froze the activities and powers of the Meriden Housing Development Commission, budget disputes with city department heads, boisterous city council meetings and continued arbitrary decisionmaking.

Grossman's second term further tarnished his reputation among the people of Meriden, ultimately serving as a catalyst for the shift from a popularly elected mayor to a city manager form of local government. Local businessman Walter A. Evilia succeeded Grossman as Meriden mayor. Although Evilia's administration followed up on some positive plans initiated or continued under prior administrations, he struggled to restore Meriden's reputation.

At last, the city was ready for a charter revision. The excesses of Mayor Abraham Grossman's last year in office were the straws that broke the camel's back. He had angered almost everyone. In blistering council meetings, which often lasted up to six hours, the mayor was charged with making unilateral decisions without council input, consent or support. Twice he was censured—the first time in history such action was approved—and twice he managed to win the mayoral vote of the people.

It was time for a change. Former mayors of both parties, city councilors and citizens at large rallied together to put forth a referendum calling for a

Mayour Walter Evilia, a Republican and a former State Representative, was the last popularly elected mayor (until a later charter revision) in the City of Meriden. *Marna Evilia.*

new form of government. It passed by a two-to-one margin. Mayor Walter Evilia, a Republican and the last popularly elected mayor until a later charter revision in 1993, proved to be a perfect transitional leader in this new hybrid form of government.

On the morning of January 14, 1980, the new city manager–city council form of government was implemented, and Dana Miller, the city's first city manager, reported for duty. *Meriden Public Library.*

This new charter revision became law in 1979, bringing sweeping changes to the City of Meriden's bylaws. A city manager–city council form of government was established to run the city, with the council appointing a ceremonial mayor. In finance, the comptroller and treasurer positions were eliminated, the tax board became advisory to the council on fiscal matters and the budget became the responsibility of the city manager, with final approval by the council. All boards and commissions except those mandated by the state were eliminated, and new, stronger departments were established.

On the morning of January 14, 1980, the new city manager–city council form of government was implemented, and Dana Miller, the city's first city manager, reported for duty. No longer solely reliant on the mayor and city council, Meriden embraced this new era—one that allowed the city to focus on strategic planning, infrastructure development and community well-being. This also began a turbulent round of battles and debates between those who favored the new form of government and those who opposed it. Miller served until his resignation became effective on January 1, 1983; however, his tenure set the tone for subsequent city managers, emphasizing collaboration, transparency and responsiveness to residents' needs.

The charter remains the foundation for Meriden's government today.

Today, as you walk Meriden's historic streets, remember the journey—from Belcher Tavern to city hall. The city charter remains a vital thread, weaving together vision, governance and progress. As the city's history intertwines with the legacies of leaders like Abraham Grossman, the guiding principles of the city charter and the tireless efforts of city managers, each thread weaves a vibrant tapestry—a tribute to the resilience, vision and community spirit that continue to define Meriden today.

Bibliography

Books

Atwater, Francis, comp. *Centennial of Meriden, June 10-16, 1906, Report of the Proceedings, with Full Description of the Many Events of Its Successful Celebration; Old Home Week: Meriden, Conn., The "Silver City."* Journal Publishing Company, 1906.

Atwater, Francis. *Memoirs of Francis Atwater: Half-Century of Recollections of an Unusually Active Life.* Horton Printing Company, 1922.

Barber, John Warner. *John Warner Barber's Views of Connecticut Towns, 1834–36.* Acorn Club, 1990.

Bartlett, Matthew W. *Tales of the Meriden Shadowlands, Folktales of the City of Meriden, Connecticut.* Self-published, 2012.

Baur, David, and Agnes Baur. *Frederick Matzow (1861–1938), Meriden's Artist-In-Residence.* Konica Minolta Business Solutions, 2006.

Benham, Welcome E. *The Life and Writings of W.E. Benham, Containing an Account of His Early Life.* E.A. Horton & Company, 1882.

Bishop, J. Leander. *Manufacturers in Meriden.* Edward Young and Company, 1868.

Bohan, Peter J., Philip H. Hammerslough and Erin Eisenbarth. *Early Connecticut Silver, 1700–1840.* Wesleyan University Press, 1970.

Brainard, Homer, Harold Simeon Gilbert and Clarence Almon Torrey. *The Gilbert Family, Descendants of Thomas Gilbert, 1582(?)–1659 of Mt. Wollaston (Braintree), Windsor, and Wethersfield.* A.C. Gilbert Company, 1953.

Breckenridge, Frances A. *Recollections of a New England Town.* Journal Publishing Company, 1899.

Burpee, Charles W. *Burpee's The Story of Connecticut.* Vols. 1–2. American Historical Company, 1939.

Cable, Mary. *The Blizzard of '88.* Macmillan Publishing, 1988.

Capstone Press Geography Department. *Connecticut, Revised and Updated.* Capstone Press, 2003.

Clark, George L. *A History of Connecticut, Its People and Institutions.* Knickerbocker Press, 1914.

Crofut, Florence S. Marcy. *Guide to the History and the Historic Sites of Connecticut.* Yale University Press, 1937.

Curtis, George Munson. *Early Silver of Connecticut and Its Makers.* International Silver Company, 1913.

Davis, Charles Henry Stanley, MD. *History of Wallingford, Conn. From Its Settlement in 1670 to the Present Time: Including Meriden, Which Was One of Its Parishes until 1806, and Cheshire, Which Was Incorporated in 1780.* Self-published, 1870.

DeForest, John W. *History of the Indians of Connecticut from the Earliest Known Period to 1850.* W. Jas. Hamersley, 1852.

DeLuca, Dan W. *The Old Leather Man, Historical Accounts of a Connecticut and New York Legend.* Wesleyan University Press, 2008.

Dockery, Patricia Williams. *Slavery and the African American Story.* Crown Books for Young Readers, 2023.

Franco, Janice Leach. *Meriden.* Images of America. Arcadia Publishing, 2010.

Gallaudet, Thomas Hopkins. *The Mother's Primer, to Teach Her Child Its Letters and How to Read: Designed Also for the Lowest Class in Primary Schools, on a New Plan.* Spalding & Storrs, 1839.

Gillespie, C.B., comp. *Art Souvenir Edition of The Meriden Daily Journal Illustrating the City of Meriden, Connecticut, in the Year 1895.* Journal Publishing Company, 1895.

Gillespie, Charles Bancroft, and George Munson Curtis. *A Century of Meriden: A Historic Record and Pictorial Description of the Town of Meriden, Connecticut and the Men Who Made It, from Earliest Settlement to Close of Its First Century of Incorporation.* Journal Publishing Company, 1906.

Hale, Clarence E. *Tales of Old Wallingford, 1670–1970.* Pequot Press, 1971.

Harling, Frederick, and Martin Kaufman. *The Ethnic Contribution to the American Revolution.* Westfield Bicentennial Committee and the Historical Journal of Western Massachusetts, 1976.

Harte, Charles Rufus. *Connecticut's Iron and Copper. 60th Annual Report of the Connecticut Society of Civil Engineers*. Privately printed, 1944.
Hasse, William F., Jr. *The History of Money and Banking in Connecticut*. Privately printed, 1957.
Hogan, Edmund P. *An American Heritage: A Book About the International Silver Company. International Silver Historical Collection.* Taylor Publishing Company, 1977.
Hubbard, Walter. *Hubbard Park*. Self-published, 1900.
Hughes, Arthur H., and Morse Allen. *Connecticut Place Names*. Connecticut Historical Society, 1976.
Jenkins, Stephen. *The Old Boston Post Road*. Knickerbocker Press, 1913.
Jenkinson, Matthew. *Charles I's Killers in America, The Lives & Afterlives of Edward Whalley & William Goffe*. Oxford University Press, 2019.
Jette, Mark. *Century of Golf in Meriden 1898–1999*. Self-published, 1999.
Kilbourne, Frederick W. *A History of St. Andrew's Parish, 1789–1939*. Vestry of St. Andrew's Parish, 1939.
King, Roger W. *Connie Mack's First Pro Game*. Bayberry Hill Press, 1978.
Lambert, Edward R. *History of the Colony of New Haven, Before and After the Union with Connecticut*. Hitchcock & Stafford, 1838.
Lieb, Frederick G. *Connie Mack, Grand Old Man of Baseball*. G.P. Putnam's Sons, 1945.
May, Earl Chapin. *Century of Silver, 1847–1947, Connecticut Yankees and a Noble Metal*. Robert M. McBride & Company, 1947.
Meriden Anti-Slavery Society. *An Apology for Abolitionists, Addressed by the Anti-Slavery Society of Meriden, Conn.; to Their Fellow-Citizens*. C.H. Pelton Printing, 1837.
Meriden Public Library/Meriden Bicentennial Committee. *Meriden at 200: A Half-Century of Change*. City of Meriden, 2006.
Meriden, the "Silver City": Connecticut Tercentenary, 1635–1935. Meriden Tercentenary Committee, 1935.
Morgan, Forrest. *Connecticut as a Colony and as a State, or One of the Original Thirteen*. Vols. 1–4. Publishing Society of Connecticut, 1904.
Pagliuco, Christopher. *The Great Escape of Edward Whalley and William Goffe: Smuggled Through Connecticut*. The History Press, 2012.
Percival, James Gates. *Report on the Geology of the State of Connecticut*. Osborn & Baldwin, Printers, 1842.
Perkins, G.W. *Historical Sketches of Meriden*. Franklin E. Hinman, 1849.
Piccirillo, Justin. *Art and Artisans of Meriden*. Arcadia Publishing, 2023.
———. *Hubbard Park*. Images of America. Arcadia Publishing, 2021.
Rainwater, Dorothy T., and Judy Renfield. *Encyclopedia of American Silver Manufacturers*. 4th rev. ed. Schiffer Publishing, 1998.

Rennison, Carter L. *The Story of the Mother Goose Farm*. Self-published, 1966.

Robillard, Ron. *Sweet Success: A History of Thompson's Candy*. Thompson Candy Company, 1997.

Rockey, John L. *History of New Haven County, Connecticut*. W.W. Preston and Company, 1892.

Rovinsky, Bruce. *The Schools of Meriden, Connecticut: A Comprehensive History, 1773–2013*. Self-published, 2014.

Shelberg, Bernice Schenk. *Solomon's House in the Woods*. Distaff Publishing, 1999.

Shipton, Clifford K. *New England Life in the 18th Century: Representative Biographies from Sibley's Harvard Graduates*. Belknap Press of Harvard University Press, 1963.

Stiles, Ezra. *A History of Three of the Judges of King Charles I. Major General Whalley, Major-General Goffe, and Colonel Dixwell; Who, at the Restoration, 1660, Fled to America; and Were Secreted and Concealed in Massachusetts and Connecticut, for Nearly Thirty Years*. Elisha Babcock, 1794.

Strother, Horatio T. *The Underground Railroad in Connecticut*. Wesleyan University Press, 1962.

Tomlinson, R.G. *Witchcraft Trials of Connecticut: The First Comprehensive, Documented History of Witchcraft Trials in Colonial Connecticut*. Connecticut Research, 1978.

Walsh, J. Leigh. *Connecticut Pioneers in Telephony: The Origin and Growth of the Telephone Industry in Connecticut*. Morris F. Tyler Chapter, Telephone Pioneers of America, 1950.

Wendover, Sanford H. *150 Years of Meriden: Published in Connection with the Observance of the City's Sesquicentennial, June 17–23, 1956*. Meriden Sesquicentennial Committee, 1956.

Images

Bains News Service, P. (between ca. 1915 and ca. 1920) Ella W. Wilcox, [Between Ca. 1915 and Ca. 1920] [1 negative : glass ; 5 x 7 in. or smaller.] Retrieved from the Library of Congress, LC-DIG-ggbain-29644 (digital file from original negative), LC-B2- 5060-14 [P&P].

Bain News Service, P. (ca. 1920) Ponselle - "Roi D'ys". , ca. 1920. [Between and Ca. 1925] [Photograph] Retrieved from the Library of Congress, https://www.loc.gov/item/2014713981/.

National Archives. "Office Files of Frederick W. Wile." Meriden Campaign.

National Archives. "Office Files of John F. Kinerk." Meriden Program.

Manuscripts and Articles

Arms, H. Phelps. "Hubbard Park, Meriden, Connecticut." *Connecticut Magazine*, February 1899.

Connecticut State Library. Connecticut School for Boys Records, RG178_001. Hartford, Connecticut. https://cslarchives.ctstatelibrary.org.

———. Revolutionary War Documents, vol. 7, pages 130–81. Hartford, Connecticut.

Gardner, Warren F. "Of All Things." *Record-Journal* (Meriden, CT), August 31, 1979–August 11, 1992.

Olmsted, John C., Firm of Olmsted Brothers, Landscape Artists. *Olmsted Letters, Hubbard Park, Meriden, Conn.* Brookline, Massachusetts, 1898.

Pynchon, W.H.C. "The Black Dog." *Connecticut Quarterly* 4 (January 1898): 153.

Silliman, Benjamin. *American Journal of Science and Arts*, October 1821. Yale University. New Haven, Connecticut.

U.S. Congress. *Memorial Services. 79th Cong., 1st. sess., 1945*. Government Printing Office, 1945.

About the Author

Jennifer Piccirillo.

Author Justin Piccirillo has spent a career in education. Upon graduating from Southern Connecticut State University, Piccirillo began a long tenure as a public school art educator. While illustrating a children's book about Meriden's Hubbard Park, Piccirillo became passionate about the city's past and has since penned numerous writings on Meriden history. These include books *Hubbard Park* (Images of America) and *Art and Artisans of Meriden*, both by Arcadia Publishing, and several articles for many regional newspapers and magazines. Today, Piccirillo continues to teach while taking an active role within the Meriden Historical Society and other Meriden-based organizations.

Piccirillo lives in Meriden with his wife, Jennifer, and three sons, Clay, Adam and Anders, and their families.